Praise for The Seven

Dr. Wesley has drawn the blueprint for a restoration project of the deacon ministry. Cutting through ministry walls decayed by time and tradition, personality and preference, *The Seven* restores God's original design for this servant office. Grounded in Scripture, supported through the testimonies of godly men, this valuable resource will bless new and seasoned ministers, as well as laity, for many years to come.

Dr. Brian E. Nall, Executive Director
Pensacola Bay Baptist Association

Thanks to Lonnie Wesley, a topic that has been cloaked in tradition in the African-American church has been brought into the light: the role of deacons. In fact, *The Seven* shines a floodlight on what Scripture says about a biblically-functioning deacon. Instead of following the spirit of the age, where deacons become powerbrokers of the church, Lonnie calls for pastors and leaders to reexamine and embrace the biblical pattern of deacons as laid out in God's Word. What is more, he describes how he walked his church though improving and developing their deacon ministry by way of discipleship, biblical training, and preaching. I am grateful to see this resource available and believe that those who follow the pattern of deacons as laid out in the Holy Scriptures will experience the advance of the gospel and unity of the faith. *Soli deo Gloria*

Brian J. Wright
Author of several best-selling books including *The Rhythm of the Christian Life, Inspired Questions,* and *Communal Reading in the Time of Jesus.*

The Seven provides a comprehensive vision of the role of deacons, focusing on the role of deacon as God's servant in the church. Letting go of power, in the spirit of Philippians 2:5-11, deacons set the table for effective worship, ministry, mission, and pastoral care. Although Lonnie Davis Wesley III and I come from very different ethnic, theological, and denominational locations, I found this text helpful in understanding the dynamics of African-American congregations and in deepening my knowledge of the role of the deacon in the early church.

Bruce Epperly
Pastor, professor, author of *Church Ahead: Moving Forward in Congregational Spiritual Practices*

Dr. Lonnie D. Wesley III has written a must-read for all Christians and anyone serving in the Deacon ministry. He provides a practical, biblically based model every deacon should inspire to become. Being a deacon myself, I've found that this piece of work has been very beneficial to my growth as a deacon. Every congregation should take advantage of this opportunity to learn and develop the skills needed to fulfill the position of deacon. May it bless you as much as it has blessed me!"

Steven D. Franklin, Deacon

The Seven

Taking a Closer Look
at What It Means to Be a Deacon

Lonnie Davis Wesley, III

Energion Publications
Gonzalez, Florida
2020

Copyright © 2020, Pens and Pins, LLC

Scripture taken from the New King James Version. Copyright © 1982 by Thomas Nelson, Inc. Used by permission. All rights reserved.

Cover Design: Henry Neufeld
Cover Picture: Lonnie Davis Wesley, III

ISBN: 978-1-63199-501-9
eISBN: 978-1-63199-508-8
Library of Congress Control Number: 2020941138

Energion Publications
P. O. Box 841
Gonzalez, Florida 32560

energion.com
pubs@energion.com

DEDICATION

I dedicate this manuscript to my Lord and Savior Jesus Christ, and I pray that this work brings glory to His kingdom. I dedicate this project to my wife, LaTonya, who patiently encourages me thoroughly through each life challenge. Additionally, I dedicate this to my daughter, Kalen, and to my sons, Jeffrey and James, for their patience while this work took me away from spending time with them. Furthermore, I dedicate this to the Greater Little Rock Baptist Church whom I have served as pastor since 2004. You are truly a jewel. Lastly, my father, L. D. Wesley, Sr., has my highest respect. He faithfully served alongside deacons for over 52 years, doing his best to help them fulfill their God-given roles as deacons. My mother, Osie Mae Wesley, went home to be with the Lord when I was 13. I pray Momma would have been proud of this effort.

In all my years as a pastor, there have been three men to serve alongside me in the position of Deacon Ministry Leader. In my opinion, Sutter Smith, Willie C. Dean, and James Myatt all have set the standard for deacons to follow. Humility in strength is the common denominator of these gentlemen. I know they have obtained for themselves a good standing, and great boldness in the faith, which is in Christ Jesus. I thank God for, and I also dedicate this work to them.

ACKNOWLEDGEMENTS

This book would not have been possible without the support of the Dean and Professors of The Clamp Divinity School of Anderson University (AU). Each professor during my time of study poured profusely into me, thus aiding in the birth of this project. I thank you.

Not only did the servants of Clamp/AU provide assistance, but appreciation is also extended to Dr. John Henry Williams, Jr., and to Dr. Sandra Winborne for reading and advising from their personal perspectives. Also, when to it came to clerical assistance, Marcia Knight was always willing and ready to lend her professional expertise. I cannot thank the three of you enough.

Lastly, personal appreciation is extended to Dr. Kris Barnett for working with and supporting this thought, and a very special personal appreciation to Dr. James Noble for his patience, direction, feedback, and encouragement along this journey.

Table of Contents

	From the Publisher	ix
	Foreword	xiii
1	God's Magnificent Plan	1
2	The Plan in Scripture and Theology	17
3	The Plan in the Experience of the African-American Church	41
4	Intentionally Preaching God's Plan	55
5	Evaluating Your Work: Are You on God's Plan?	69

Teaching God's Plan to the Church

"The Results of Helping the Pastor" 75
"What the Deacon – and Everybody - Should Know" 83
"Thank God for the Deacon" 93
"When Serving Meets Persecution" 101

Bibliography 109

From the Publisher

How to Use This Book

You will find that this book is arranged a bit differently than you might expect. The publishers and author have chosen to present everything necessary to study, implement, and support an improved deacon ministry in your church in one volume. This means you will only need this one volume in order to develop your deacon ministry

Here are some of the potential users.

Pastors, along with members of the church leadership team

If you are a pastor or are working with the pastor as part of the leadership team, it would be a good idea to read and study the entire book. Reforming the deacon ministry of your church will require you to understand where you are going and communicate that to your church. This book grew out of experience strengthened and organized by study which resulted in success. The introduction and the first three chapters will provide the background. The Project Evaluation chapter will give you an idea of what changes to look for in the attitudes of church members. The four sermons show you how the author, in his church and using his discernment, presented this message. Prayerfully make the message your own and create your own educational plan for the congregation. You will find resources, including a week-long teaching plan and a questionnaire for deacon candidates available free of charge on the publishers web site: https://energion.com/deacons.

Don't plan to borrow the sermons in this book. Look at the picture behind the section heading. That's Greater Little Rock Baptist Church. That's not the church God gave *you* to steward for him. Learn what you need to learn and then prepare your series of sermons so as to reach the people of your church.

Deacon candidates

You need to study the introduction and first three chapters. Your pastor and leadership team will provide you with their program for training. It may be precisely like the one in this book, or may include other information as they discern their need. Start out ready to learn and adapt.

Family members of deacon candidates

Be prepared to support the candidate in prayer, and to study along as he prepares. A great deal of what you need to know is contained in the sermons in the back of the book. They will make good reading for you, but make sure also to listen to your pastor as he preaches and teaches on this topic.

Every church member

Look at the introduction and the first three chapters, then read the sermons. Listen as your pastor and leadership team teach you. Pray for them and encourage them.

Foreword

The Word of God informs us that there are two biblical officers in the New Testament church, pastors and deacons. While many of us if not most of us understand the role of the pastor, unfortunately, the same cannot be said of the role of the deacon. Consequently, many of us have read about or even been a part of churches where chaos, confusion, and cliques have caused havoc, mess, ungodliness and even church splits because of the misunderstood role of deacons. I saw this first hand in the church I grew up in as a teenager. I remember vividly shouts, arguments and even some physical altercations between deacons, pastors, and other members of the church! I knew then as I know now that this should not be the behavior of church leaders.

So, what's the answer? What's the remedy? How should the church address this ungodly behavior? How do we stop this misunderstanding of the role of deacons in the New Testament church? How can we counterattack this spiritual warfare that has been affecting churches for generations? Well, you hold the answer in your hands.

In his very informative and inspirational book, "The Seven," my friend and brother Dr. Lonnie Wesley, after months of interviews, phone calls and research has given us some practical principles of the Biblical role of deacons as God first designed and desired when the apostles first appointed seven men of good reputation, full of the Holy Spirit and wisdom, to assist in the work of the ministry in Acts Chapter 6. Each chapter of this book will offer you information and insight on how deacons should fulfill their roles so that the members of the church could benefit.

As an added bonus, Dr. Wesley includes several sermons he preached from the pulpit he pastors at Greater Little Rock Baptist Church dealing with the topic of deacons. Finally, as the son of a pastor, and even as a former deacon himself, the author offers personal experience to his desire of wanting to see deacons fulfill their Biblical role in the church.

Thank you, Dr. Wesley for your timely book, "The Seven." Pastors, deacons, and churches will certainly benefit from what you share.

Pastor Fred Luter, Jr.
Franklin Avenue Baptist Church
New Orleans, Louisiana
Former President
Southern Baptist Convention

CHAPTER ONE:
GOD'S MAGNIFICENT PLAN

Why write about deacons? I wrote this for several reasons. The first reason is to document what the Bible says about the role of a deacon, and then compare that to the prevailing definition of how that ministry functions within the local association of churches, the First West Florida Baptist District Association. The second reason I wrote this is to research and reveal the Biblical history of the role of the deacon. The opportunity to examine the complicated relationship of the African American pastor and his deacon throughout history is the third reason. The fourth reason is to provide educational opportunities for Believers to learn how the Biblical role of a deacon should function.

To satisfy the first concern, the intent is to juxtapose the current thinking on the ministry of deacons with what the Bible teaches on ministry of the deacon. Acts 6:1–7 and 1 Timothy 3:8–13 will be the primary Scripture passages used to develop the Biblical understanding of the deacon ministry.

As previously stated, the second reason this was written was to highlight the Biblical history of the deacon. Included within this is the origin and history of current congregational thinking as it relates to the Biblical history of the deacon. To provide a compelling argument on the relationship between the pastor and deacon, Joe McKeever, a noted pastor and author says:

> Deacons and pastors are partners. Deacons follow the leadership of the pastor. When they cease to do that, the system breaks down. My favorite analogy for the working relationship of pastor and deacons comes from the Old West where the cowboys would move the herd to the railhead. Out in front of the herd, the pastor rides point. He sets the directions. On the sides, someone of his designation – usually other ministers – ride flank. They keep the herd together and keep them moving toward the goal. And in the back, eating the dust of the entire group, the deacons ride drag. The root of *diakonos* is literally, "through the dust." So, our analogy of deacons as the ones riding drag has good precedence. Those cowhands are usually the youngest or newest or the ones in trouble with the boss, because this is the dirtiest, and hardest work of all.[1]

McKeever's thoughts are even more motivation for this book, but with one exception. My experience has been that sometimes the cowhand in the back riding drag (the deacon) will draw his gun and shoot the cowboy riding point (the pastor) in the back. This is what I have seen, firsthand. Sometimes one wonders if the cowboys were working the same herd for the same owner. It is believed that this is the kind of ecclesial crime that preaching and teaching can fix and prevent.

Included within this second goal of the study is to show where the deacon originates Biblically, while simultaneously showing where he originates practically within the context and culture of the African American church. Showing this should challenge the understanding of the Church regarding how the deacon ministry is expected to function in today's congregation.

To satisfy the third reason for writing, I must show you how the African American pastor-deacon relationship has a deep and complicated history. Born out of slavery's demise, the Historic

---

1 Joe McKeever, *Help! I'm a Deacon!* (Cleveland, Tennessee: Parson's Porch & Company, 2015), p. 135.

The Seven

John the Baptist Church of Pensacola, Florida, and the Terry Grove Baptist Church of Terry, Mississippi, are wonderful microcosms of the earliest history of the Baptist denomination of the African American church.[2] These early beginnings illustrate how the pastor-deacon dynamic originated. By looking into the history of these two congregations, it is believed we will see exactly how the role of the deacon in these two African American congregations evolved into an unbiblical nature, and give reasons why many other congregations fell into the same situation. The evolution of the deacon relates to the second reason of my writing inasmuch as the relationship between the African American deacon and his pastor evolved as a sure by-product from her unintended/unplanned birth.

It is practical to assume that African Americans struggled with reading during the late 1860s. If so, then where did the Black Church get her cues as to how to serve or work in the church? Who taught her? Whom did she watch? These questions, and more, are asked and answered in this project by understanding the pastor-deacon relationship in the Black Church. Does that relationship line up with Scripture? If so, how does this relationship shape the thought pattern of what the deacon is?

The fourth and final reason for writing this venture is to highlight Biblical qualifications and instructions for deacons. I believe the first way to accomplish this is through preaching the gospel, utilizing the expository preaching method. Through my study of the subject, the second way for me to highlight the Biblical qualifications and instructions for deacons was by leading various training sessions. Scriptures pertaining to the ministry of deacons were expounded upon in each class for current and prospective deacons. These teaching opportunities originated through workshops from the ministries of the First West Florida Baptist District Association, such as the Congress of Christian Education, the Ushers, Laymen, and Choir Winter Institute and the Women's Department. The "parent body" of the Association also offers such teaching opportunities.

---

2   Historic John the Baptist Church, History, accessed February 20, 2017, http://historicjohnthebaptist.blogspot.com.

The congregations that comprise the First West Florida Baptist District Association send congregants to attend the aforementioned learning opportunities. Therefore, those that the congregations select to attend at a future date are enrolled in the deacon class for training. More specifically stated, usually during the third week of the month of May (annually), the Congress of Christian Education (the education wing of the Association) meets for five days of intensive learning. Of the eight to ten classes offered, one of them is a class entitled "Becoming an Effective Deacon." This is an opportunity to share with more than Greater Little Rock Baptist Church, effectively touching multiple congregations of the association. Each class lasts for one hour and 15 minutes for five days (Monday – Friday).

The same teaching opportunities are available during the third week in July (the annual association week) and the third week in January (the annual Ushers, Laymen, and Choir Winter Institute). The Baptist Center, in Pensacola, Florida, holds these seminars. Pastors, along with current and future deacons are welcome to attend these classes.

In addition to annual associational chances, I am also blessed to receive opportunities to teach/train current and perspective deacons through invitations from pastors. The foundation of the deacon training is Acts 6:1–7. Although the men of Acts 6 were not deacons, it is widely believed that they were the forerunners of deacons and, as a result, their origin and specificity of service is used in the training as examples of deacons-in-action. In *Handbook for Deacons*, J. D. O'Donnell makes it plain:

> The story of Acts 6:1-8 is generally alluded to as the first election of deacons. Indeed, it must be looked upon as the origin of the office even though the men were not called deacons nor conceived to be such at this time. The seven men in Acts 6 were selected to perform a certain mechanical or secondary task. This task had to do with the distribution of material benefits to fill the needs of the widows in the Jerusalem church. The apostles were becoming weighed down with these secondary tasks and felt that more important functions demanded their attention.

Therefore, seven men were chosen to minister to the needs of the widows while the apostles gave themselves "continually to prayer, and to the ministry of the word."[3]

O'Donnell goes on to say that, "The election of the seven men in Acts 6 was probably the forerunner of the office of deacon. These men were chosen to perform a special task – to care for the widows."[4] In his work, *The Work of the Deacon and Deaconess*, which has sold more than a million copies, Harold Nichols teaches that:

> At the request of the apostles, the early church selected 'seven men of good standing, full of the Spirit and of wisdom, whom we may appoint to this task' (Acts 6:3). The duty? To serve the daily needs of the people, especially those who might otherwise be marginalized or neglected. (In the inaugural diaconate, the priority task was ensuring that the distribution of resources to Gentile widows in the faith community was equal to those received by the Jewish widows.) These first deacons shared the burden of congregational ministry so that the spiritual leaders, the apostles, could focus their attention on the task of preaching and teaching the new community of disciples. Many other places throughout the New Testament make references to various kinds of services to be performed.[5]

---

3 J. D. O'Donnell, *Handbook for Deacons* (Nashville, Tennessee: Randall House, 1973), 9.
4 Ibid, 10.
5 Harold Nichols, *The Work of the Deacon and Deaconess* (Valley Forge, PA: Judson Press, 1984), 1.

INTRODUCTION AND HISTORY OF PROBLEM

Is the role of deacons in congregations today becoming something other than what the Bible intended? If so, neither history nor Biblical tradition will support any non-biblical description or expectation of the deacon of the African American church in the Baptist denomination. If true, both pastor and congregation will continue to suffer, resulting in a deadly domino effect in the body of Christ and in the communities, therefore, the people will be left under-served. Wherefore, finding herself mired in such a non-biblical tradition, how did the Church (the universal church) get this way?

Tucked within the history of Terry Grove Missionary Baptist Church of Terry, Mississippi lies a possible solution. Terry Grove is not unlike many African American churches in the southern region of the United States. Actually, except for her age, Terry Grove mirrors many Black Baptist congregations inasmuch as the struggle to survive has given rise to many current-day misconceptions, which in turn, have become constant realities.

With a rich history, orally passed down from generation to generation, Terry Grove Baptist Church started in 1865, just months after the Civil War ended. Having a church meeting was extremely difficult for Black people to do at this time, as Blacks could not worship God freely. Plantation owners outlawed larger gatherings of Blacks.

The Reverend Marion Dunbar, a freed slave, was the very first pastor of what would become Terry Grove. For that time, Dunbar's God-given vision for the people of God stretched far and wide. Court records, land tracts and certain historical events indicate that he and his six followers organized the first church around 1865; however, the church origin is traced back to events growing out of and before the Civil War and Reconstruction Eras. Before and during the Civil War, Blacks held church services in secret if they wanted to practice their religious traditions. Religion grew to become a highly respected part of slave life. It offered hope and reassurance that brighter days were to come. Held after dark, these meetings carried on late into the night. The locations would vary so that getting caught was less likely.

Reverend Dunbar and his six followers erected the first structure of what would become the Terry Grove church. This building was a brush harbor (or brush arbor). A brush harbor is a temporary structure made of tree limbs bound together and covered with brushes and bushes. On the church property, it provided the shade, the cover and the walls. Chicken wire was also used to help hold the structure together. The land belonged to a White family, and they deeded the land to the members of Terry Grove. Soon after receiving the deed, members built the first wooden structure.[6]

So as not to give the impression that this phenomenon did not happen in other areas of the country, I would also like to highlight the Historic John the Baptist Church. Pensacola, Florida, is the birthplace of the Historic John the Baptist Church, a birth which took place an astounding 19 years before Terry Grove was born. In 1846, Historic John the Baptist first endured the name of the First Baptist Colored Church of Pensacola. Both freed people and slaves erected the church at Seville Square in Pensacola.

Before the Civil War, slaves and slave masters worshipped together at this church; however, during the war a conflict developed between the White members and the Black members. When rumor of burning the town spread, everyone fled war-torn Pensacola all except 72 Whites and 10 Blacks. Most of these people took the train to Greenville, Alabama, where the government of Pensacola operated in exile. When the war ended in 1865, many people eventually returned to Pensacola. While all of the White churches locked their doors, the 10 blacks who remained kept the doors opened at the church. It was in this way that the First Baptist Colored Church was the lone Civil War survivor of Pensacola's Protestant churches.

Moreover, these Black Baptists encountered problems when the Florida territorial law enabled the newly organized White Baptist

---

6   Terry Grove Missionary Baptist Church, Church History, accessed October 2018, http://www.terrygrovechurch.org/church-history.html.

Church to take control of the church. The law required that White trustees must oversee Black churches and prohibited Blacks from assembling without the presence of a White man. The law brought a monumental change to Pensacola where little slavery had existed. In fact, many runaway slaves sought freedom in Spanish Pensacola.[7] Many of the Black Baptists had become property owners. Free blacks enjoyed almost as much freedom as Whites. Pensacola was once a land of freedom within a land of slavery.

By 1847, White Americans from Alabama organized Pensacola Baptist Church in Christ, the original name of First Baptist Church Pensacola. These White Baptists moved into the black Baptist Church. Eventually, the White trustees took complete control of the black Baptist Church. Ownership of the property became theirs when the White trustees recorded their name on the colored church's deed. Documentation of colored ownership of the Baptist Church of Seville Square shows in an 1856 Freedmen's Bureau letter that the National Archives kept as public records. The members of the Historic John the Baptist Church erected the building in 1872, at the corner of 10th Avenue and Salamanca Street. John the Baptist is the oldest black Baptist church in Pensacola and in Escambia County, Florida.[8]

Just like Terry Grove in Mississippi, the Florida-based John the Baptist Church endured many challenges and changes through the years brought on by her fight to survive. For one, at John the Baptist, just like at Terry Grove, pastoral leadership was part-time at best. Since Black churches were few, the Black church did not meet for worship service every Sunday. The preacher would often split his time serving as many congregations as he humanly could. This practice still exists today. The preacher may be at "Church A" on the first Sunday of the month and he can be at "Church B" on the second Sunday and so on, often being at a different church

---

[7] Historic John the Baptist Church, History, http://www.historicjohnthebaptist.blogspot.com/p/church-history.html.

[8] Historic John the Baptist Church, History, http://www.historicjohnthebaptist.blogspot.com/p/church-history.html.

each week of the month. These congregations would be too poor to pay the preacher in money, so they often paid him in food or in a combination of both food and money.

While the preacher was away from the congregation, someone had to be in charge, and that someone was the deacon. Since the offices of pastor and deacon are the only two offices found in Scripture for the church, it made sense to view the deacon as second in command. In the absence of the pastor, the deacon started and ended the worship service. The deacon lived in the community where the church was located. The pastor lived elsewhere and traveled to the church. The time and temperature of society dictated that the community of the Black church needed a leader. The deacon was there to lead. And, as an entire county of Black churches was born out of both John the Baptist and Terry Grove in their respective communities, so was the idea that the deacon had power and privilege equal to that of the pastor.

Because of the racist climate in which the Black church initially found herself, the man of every Black household was not respected as a man outside of his house. My father, L. D. Wesley, Sr, and my uncle, Hosea Montgomery, Jr, would share with me of how Whites would look at them as "boys," at best. My father, especially, would share how White men spat on, slapped, refused service, and falsely accused Black men.

But in the confines of the church, the Black deacon found a place where he stood taller than everyone else. The church members respected him. He could speak his mind there. He could exercise authority there. He was the man there.

There were three people, all men, in the Black community who demanded instant respect. By virtue of their positions, they commanded attention at every corner of the Black community. Those positions were the mortician, the educator, and the preacher.

On Sunday morning before speaking, the preacher had to wait for the Chairman of the Deacon Board to finish the devotion period. The devotion period is when the deacon calls the people to order, lines the hymn, prays a prayer and sings a song. This process kept the deacon in front of the people. The deacon had a platform. He had attention. He had a stage and was in charge. The deacon (again, usually the Chairman of the Deacon Board) took up the offering. He counted the money at church, collected it from home-bound members, and transported it to the church. The Chairman of the Deacon Board was clearly and unquestionably in charge.

Dr. Jerry Young, the current President of the National Baptist Convention, leads over 30,000 congregations with more than 7 million members, but he also has personal experience with the non-fulltime church. Dr. Young has been around long enough to see the effects of the misplaced ideals of the deacon in a ministry:

> I came out of Greenville, Mississippi, and I was pastor of two churches in Greenville. And, in those churches, I had tremendous conflict with the Deacon Board – in both churches. In one church, in particular, it was just horrific. Long meetings, a lot of bickering and it was just horrible; and in terms of the relationship…there is absolutely no question that what happens in so many of our churches is antithetical to the biblical concept of what it means to be a deacon. And so, that is the absolute case. (And) It is unfortunate, but the idea of "Deacon Board" has created, in my opinion, the greatest hindrance because the concept of "Board" is a secular concept. People who serve on Boards in corporations and things like that, they see themselves as bosses. They see themselves as being in control, and that same concept, literally, crept into the church where the deacons said, "We are the Board," and they actually felt like that meant, "We're in charge of this church." Which is totally antithetical, not only to the biblical concept of deacons, but to Baptist church polity. And, so, there's a tremendous conflict. But that idea of "Board," I mean…and there were guys who simply said, "We are the Board…our job is to run this church. Our job is the keep the pastor under control. Our job is to do this…" Because they saw themselves, literally, as a Board and as a Board of Directors, as opposed to servants who are a part of the diaconate…they saw no relationship to that.[9]

---

9   Personal interview, "Jerry Young" September 2018

Out of personal experience, Dr. Young speaks to the detriment of misplaced titles, which leads to misplaced expectations.

Background from Personal Perspective

Like Dr. Young, I am also the son of a pastor. As such, I know that many pastor-deacon fight stories happened on a weekly basis (first-hand accounts directly from the pastor, and second-hand accounts from the friends of the pastor). For 27 of his 52-year pastoral career, my father was simultaneously the pastor of two congregations – again, like Dr. Young. With this double pastoral assignment, there was never a deficiency of pastor-deacon fight stories and of stories about how the pastor and deacon would argue in church.

Some stories that are never forgotten include the story of the pastor who pulled a knife on the deacon after a church business meeting. Frustration had finally set in on the pastor past the point of him being able to control it. He was tired of the actions that the Deacon Board Chairman led. And then there is the story of the deacon who got caught stealing money from the church, framed the pastor, and eventually had the pastor voted out of the church.

Although these stories happened in Pensacola, Florida, stories of this nature are not limited to this region. Dr. Fred Luter, the past President of the Southern Baptist Convention, has visited numerous congregations around the country and has heard numerous stories… just like this one.

> The deacon position and his role has fallen into an unbiblical model. Unfortunately, now in many of our churches in America, deacons – their role – they seem (to think that) they are in charge of the church. There is always tension between the deacons and the pastor; they are always trying to run things. That has never been the deacon's role, according to Scripture. So, to answer your question, yes, I believe the role has fallen. I think when we started doing these constitutions and by-laws, and got away from what the Bible says, it just changed the role

of a deacon. In my position of the President of the Southern Baptist Convention, I dealt with a whole lot of churches, and I will never forget talking to a pastor who was just crushed because a handful of deacons of the church voted him out, while the membership wanted him to stay, but the constitution gave the deacons that power. And so, even though the majority of the membership still wanted him, the deacons voted him out. And that's just unbiblical. That's not what the role of the deacon was supposed to be, according to the Book of Acts. So, I think, when we started putting together these constitutions...I know we need them legally for churches (but) when we started doing these constitutions and by-laws and allowing Roberts Rule of Order to conduct our business, then I think we got off track.[10]

Additionally, I want to give some highlights from serving as a deacon. Because of this experience, I can unequivocally say that I believe many deacons believe they, indeed, oversee the church. This mentality dictates both their words and actions. Again, being the son of the pastor of the church afforded the opportunity to see, hear and be a part of more than the average church member. As time moved on, it became easier to see vast differences between what was expected of the deacon in this church atmosphere and what a more Biblical perspective of a deacon should be. These differences led to unnecessary congregational problems.

Charles W. Deweese teaches about deacons using sources from the second through the fifth centuries. He said,

> These sources show that early deacons had duties relating to charity, administration, education, and worship. To begin with, deacons did pastoral work through being the real agents of charity for the church. They visited martyrs who were in prison, clothed and buried the dead, looked after the excommunicated with the hope of restoring them, provided for the needs of widows and orphans, visited the sick and those who were otherwise in distress. In a plague that struck Alexandra about A. D. 259, deacons were described by an eyewitness

---

10   Personal interview, "Fred Luter" September 2018.

as those who "visited the sick fearlessly," "ministered to them continuously," and "died with them most joyfully."[11]

When I read the description of these deacons, of which Deweese speaks, just the thought of the action of some of those initial deacons is enough to make your head spin. The deacon of which Deweese speaks was not the prevailing deacon of my experience. The deacon that Young, Luter, and my father had to deal with was the prevailing deacon of my experience.

BACKGROUND FROM A PROFESSIONAL PERSPECTIVE

Writing this book came to mind when I was 35 years old and had just arrived at my new pastoral assignment at Greater Little Rock Baptist Church. Did I know *exactly* what to do? Of course not. I was young, Pensacola, Florida, was not Terry, Mississippi, and Greater Little Rock was not Terry Grove! Again, I was young, and I had just spent seven years as pastor of a church that had raffled off a calf to raise money to buy their Hammond B3. Although that would not end up being their norm, it was what they had to do at that time.

I shall never forget my first pastoral years at Terry Grove. God knows I loved those folks, and I loved every day I spent with them. When I first got there, Terry Grove averaged between 25–40 folks at worship services. In addition to, of course, being in a small, rural town like the Greenville church of Dr. Young's initial pastoral ministry, and like 27 of my father's 52-year pastoral career, Terry Grove only met at her facility for worship services twice a month. To be clear, Terry Grove met for Sunday Church School every Sunday, but only on the first and third Sundays of the month did the church have consistent worship service. When the fifth Sunday came around, the members would either stay home or go visit other congregations. This, or something similar, is what many of

---

11 Charles W. Deweese, *The Emerging Role of Deacons* (Nashville, Tennessee: Broadman Press, 1979).

the Black congregations did in the rural communities across the South. During that era, few churches were full-time, which is the term that is used to describe a ministry when the congregation meets every Sunday for worship services.

I was 27 when I answered the call into the preaching ministry, preaching my first public sermon. I had just gotten married 19 months earlier, and my wife and I would have our first child 10 months after that initial sermon. Five months after our daughter's arrival, Terry Grove called me to be their pastor. I was shell-shocked. Yes, I was the son of a pastor, but that is vastly different from being the pastor!

Seven years and one month after serving Terry Grove, while standing in the rear, East Hall of Greater Little Rock Baptist Church, I was shell-shocked again when a deacon pointed his right index finger about two inches away from my nose and said, "I know what you're doing! You think you're going to run this church! But...," the deacon said with a tremble in his voice, "I've got something for that!"

When the deacon uttered those words, an immediate question came to my mind: "What is the best course of action to keep this from happening again?" I reminded myself that I was serving and doing what God had told me to do for the sake of God's people. I was there to preach the Word. I was there to lead in building the kingdom of God at that location.

I thought about the pastor-deacon fights I had heard about while growing up. I entertained what the congregation thought that the Biblical mandate of the deacon was. I thought about what the deacon did (in and out of church) and the Biblical expectations of the deacon.

I also asked myself what it would take to change the pastor-deacon relationship dynamic. What would it take to change the congregational perception of the deacon? Had the Biblical light that once shined on the deacon burned out? Had the deacon lost his Biblical way? All of this rushed through my mind, trying to strategize to make sure that my pastoral career would not follow the path of my father's and many other pastors across the country.

The path that ended with the ministry being forgotten, overlooked, and unkept due to fights with the deacon.

It is not that my father did not have a successful pastoral career – he did. God blessed him with many, many more wins than losses. Any time you minister while staying ahead of the needed building program – a program that succeeded without having to borrow money to get the projects done – is classified as being successful. God constantly added souls to Pleasant Hill, and having the space needed to teach the congregation was never a problem. The Lord blessed my father. He was a successful pastor. I just could not help, however, but to wonder just how much more successful he (and the church) could have been if my father had deacons to work with him instead of fighting him at every turn.

There were more than a few squabbles with deacons. In fact, there were so many squabbles that what the deacons did was thought of as being what deacons were supposed to do. I watched deacons fight with my father, rather than work with him to better serve the congregation.

Background from a Public Perspective

The road to realizing and recovering from pastor-deacon problems in the church is not unlike addiction recovery. The Camp Recovery Center (CRC) says that the very first stage of the Five Stages of Addiction Recovery states that there must be awareness and early acknowledgement. This stage is marked by a growing awareness that there is a problem. In some cases, this realization results from conversations with family members, friends or co-workers. In some cases, addiction leads to health, financial, work or legal problems. Although the addict is still engaging in addictive behaviors and has not made any measurable progress toward ending those behaviors, this first stage is critical in paving the way for the rest of the recovery process.[12]

---

12 CRC Health, The 5 Stages of Addiction Recovery, http://www.crchealth.com, accessed October 18, 2018.

The parallel is drawn to the pastor-deacon relationship, and deacon responsibility, in order to get the ministry of deacons back on the Biblical track. To do that, someone first must admit that there is a need. We must have a growing awareness that there is a problem. There is a strong desire to give pastors and congregations access to the solutions to those problems. Saints must be equipped with the knowledge that the pastor-deacon relationship does not have to be one of contentions, filled with controversy, nor one that conforms to the standard of the world.

The news must be spread that the pastor-deacon relationship can and should be one that exemplifies Biblical standards that come from Biblical foundations that result in the Word of God going forth. Consequently, the church can focus on the Great Commission and see a great increase in the number of disciples.

CHAPTER TWO
THE PLAN IN SCRIPTURE AND THEOLOGY

There is nothing more honorable to a man than the office of a deacon or minister. We magnify our office, though we would not magnify ourselves. We hold there is nothing that can dignify a man more than being appointed to an office in the Christian church. I would rather be a deacon of a church than Lord Mayor of London. — Spurgeon[13]

Deacons hold a high position in the church. Their role demands hard work and faithful service for the overall success of the ministry. Acts 6 demonstrates the necessity of Godly men who can achieve this mission. Additionally, one of the purposes of this book is to outline what the Bible teaches about the definition and the ministry of the deacon. Acts 6 accomplishes these goals. From the beginning we learn that the church was growing, and all seemed well. After the death of Jesus, Luke wrote that Jesus returned and miraculously appeared unto His disciples for 40 days. While communing with His disciples, Christ instructed them that after the Holy Spirit comes upon them, they shall indeed be His witnesses in Jerusalem, in all Judea, in Samaria, and to the end of

---

13 Kerry James Allen, *Spurgeon's Quotes; The Definite Collection* (The Woodland, Texas, Kress Biblical Resources, 2018), M-512.

the earth. After giving these instructions, and while they watched, Jesus disappeared out of their sight by a cloud (Acts 1:4–9).

Fifty days after Passover, Pentecost found the disciples in one place when they all heard a sound like a mighty, rushing wind, as that sound filled the house. Then divided tongues appeared to them, as of fire, and one sat upon each of them, and the Holy Spirit filled them all, and they began to speak with other tongues as the Spirit gave them utterance. However, everyone heard it in their own language. After this, Peter preached resulting in about 3,000 souls being added to the church that day (Acts 2:1–41).

The apostles continued daily with one accord in the temple. The disciples would break bread from house to house, they ate and praised God together, and God added to the church daily those who were being saved. The Lord's church was growing, and all seemed well.

The early church did the work of the Lord. The apostles ministered to the community by teaching and preaching, people witnessed miracles, signs, and wonders, and the church grew. However, this growth was not without problems. That is when the internal murmuring began.

The apostles had faced external murmuring and fighting, such as the Sadducees fighting the church. The Sanhedrin had fought the church. Peter, James, John, and all of the apostles were familiar with attacks from the outside such as these, but this would be their first time having to battle an attack from the inside. This was internal murmuring so, how would they handle it? What would be their plan? How would the leaders of God's church combat this? What would be the plan of action to combat this internal assault on God's church? Dr. R. Kent Hughes sets this stage:

> When a certain Dallas church decided to split, each faction filed a lawsuit to claim the church property. A judge finally referred the matter to the higher authorities in the particular denomination. A church court assembled to hear both sides of the case and awarded the church property to one of the two

factions. The losers withdrew and formed another church in the area.

During the hearing, the church courts learned that the conflict had all begun at a church dinner when a certain elder received a smaller slice of ham than a child seated next to him. Sadly, this was reported in the newspapers for everyone to read. Just imagine how the people of Dallas laughed about that situation! This brought great discredit not only to the church but to Jesus Christ!

The tiniest events sometimes cause great problems. Repeatedly, a church has warded off a frontal attack only to be subverted from within.

Acts 6 shows us Satan trying to disrupt the inward peace of the early church. Wonderful things were happening as the new church grew rapidly. Three thousand received Christ at Pentecost. The Lord added another 2,000 shortly thereafter. Acts 5 tells us that many more were then added to the church. Satan, unhappy about God's successes, sowed a spirit of murmuring and gossip among God's people, hoping to set believer against believer.

People attempted to destroy the works of God in this way. God blesses a work, souls come to Christ, the church reaches its community, and sends out missionaries. Then someone complains that they are not appreciated or is being neglected. Perhaps this comes in the form of a critical glance, a forgotten name, a social gaffe, or some imagined offense. Bitter dissension ignites and spreads, and the whole work goes up in flames.

Acts 6 describes such a situation. The delicate unity of the early church became endangered, threatening the spiritual testimony of many thousands of believers.[14]

To handle the attack on the unity of the church, the apostles' reaction, in the form of a request of the early church, was to select "seven men of good standing, full of the Spirit and of wisdom, whom we may appoint to this task" (*Acts 6:3*). The duty was to serve the daily needs of the people, especially those who might

---

14 R. Kent Hughes *ACTS the Church Afire* (Wheaton, Illinois: Crossway Books, 1996), 93–94.

otherwise be marginalized or neglected. In the inaugural diaconate, the priority task was ensuring that the distribution of resources to Gentile widows in the faith community was equal to those that the Jewish widows received. These first deacons shared the burden of congregational ministry so that the spiritual leaders, the apostles, could focus their attention on the tasks of preaching and teaching the new community of disciples. Many other places throughout the New Testament refer to various kinds of service to be performed.

It must be pointed out that the seven individuals chosen for the special task of caring for the widows and serving tables were not specifically called deacons in Acts 6.

> The Greek noun *diakonos* (which we translate as deacon) appears in 1 Timothy 3 but not in Acts 6. Instead, it is the Greek *diakonia* that appears in Acts 6:1, and the word *diakonein* appears in Acts 6:2, both of which are verb forms. These word usages suggest an action to be taken, rather than an office or a position to be filled. In other words, first and foremost, the seven were called to perform a service, not fill an office. When the noun "deacon" is used subsequently in the New Testament, it is generally assumed that it refers to individuals who were performing service similar to that which was assigned to the original seven who were selected. This assumption seems logical when it is understood that the Greek word from which "deacon" is derived usually describes the work of a servant. Whether or not there was a difference between the tasks described in the Book of Acts and that which might be called the office of deacon in the church seems today to be inconsequential. The fact is that these people performed the work of serving; therefore, they may be called deacons, or those who serve.[15]

The story of Acts 6:1–8 alludes to the first election of deacons. Indeed, this is looked upon as the origin of the office even though the men were not called deacons nor conceived to be such at this time.

The church selected the seven men in Acts 6 to perform a certain specific, mechanical or secondary task. This task had to do with the

15 Harold Nichols, *The Work of the Deacon & Deaconess* (Valley Forge, Pennsylvania: Judson Press, 2014), 1–2.

distribution of material benefits to fill the needs of the widows in the Jerusalem church. These secondary tasks heavily weighed on the apostles, causing them to neglect their most important functions of the ministry. Therefore, seven men were chosen to minister to the needs of the widows while the apostles gave themselves "continually to prayer and to the ministry of the word" (*Acts 6:4*).[16]

Waiting on tables would have left the apostles little time for anything or anyone else. Possibly the apostles would have dried up spiritually under the pressure of serving meals plus all the counseling and preaching, with little time for preparation and prayer. Furthermore, if the apostles personally agreed to lead the food program others might have hesitated to perform the slightest ministry without apostolic direction, and that would have fostered the over-dependence we sometimes see today, with followers afraid to tie their shoes without getting permission from the pastor. Delegation is at the heart of developing followers.[17]

For some pastors today, delegating ministry involvement is no small feat. Whether there is a misguided idea of ministry glamour, or misguided ministry-minded men of which to choose from, some pastors today find it hard to delegate ministry opportunities to deacons. So, is there really any wonder when said misguided men, when they do become deacons, take the opportunity to act the way they believe a deacon should act, rather than waiting to be trained when asked to fill a ministry opportunity that may never come? In other words, should we be surprised when a ministry of deacons falls from a Biblical model to an unbiblical model? Ted Traylor, the former Vice President of the Southern Baptist Convention and current pastor of the 11,000-member Olive Baptist Church in Pensacola, when asked if he thought today's deacon ministry has fallen from a Biblical model to an unbiblical model, offered these words:

> I think there are probably two or three reasons for that. Number one, it's easier to administrate than it is to serve, and it

---

16 O'Donnell, *Handbook for Deacons*, 9.
17 R. Kent Hughes *ACTS the Church Afire* (Wheaton, Illinois: Crossway Books, 1996), 95.

takes humility to serve; it just takes arrogance to run the thing. So, it's easier on that side. Sometimes it's necessary because the pastor has not done what he should do, and the deacon has to jump in to do some things they really, probably don't want to do, but they have to carry the water because the pastor has not done that, and they have not learned to work together in doing that. So, I don't lay all that on those men, just because I think they have a spiritual issue; sometimes it's just out of necessity, just for the good of the church, that they have to step up and do some things that, otherwise, they probably wouldn't even want to do, but they have to.[18]

But the pastors of this first century church, if we can refer to the apostles as such, had served their Master wisely and skillfully. Their invitation to seek out from among the congregation seven men of good reputation, full of the Holy Spirit and wisdom, whom they may appoint over this business yielded Stephen, a man full of faith and the Holy Spirit, and Philip, Prochorus, Nicanor, Timon, Parmenas, and Nicolas, a proselyte from Antioch, whom the congregation set before the apostles (Acts 6:5).

Theologically speaking, although many may agree that the seven were not deacons but the forerunner of deacons, it is more than acceptable not only to teach deacons and the deaconship from Acts 6:1–7, but also to fuse that Scripture with 1 Timothy 3:8–13. Moreover, David Platt, Daniel L. Akin, and Tony Merida suggested taking an honest look at what these leading servants did in Acts 6 and the way they are described in 1 Timothy 3.[19] In this letter of both encouragement and instruction to Timothy, the Apostle Paul gives an official but not exhaustive list of the requirements for deacons.

NINE QUALIFICATIONS OF DEACON

After the qualifications of church overseers (bishops/elders/under-shepherds/pastors) in 1 Timothy 3:1–7, Paul then identifies

---

18 Personal Interview, "Ted Traylor," September 2018.
19 David Platt, Daniel L. Akin, and Tony Merida, *Christ-Centered Exposition: Exalting Jesus in 1 & 2 Timothy and Titus* (Nashville, Tennessee: B&H Publishing Group, 2013).

The Seven   23

nine qualifications for deacons in 3:8–12. Benjamin Merkle defines each of the nine qualifications accordingly:

1. **Dignified (v. 8):** This term normally refers to something that is honorable, esteemed, or worthy, and is closely related to "respectable," which is given as a qualification for elders (*1 Tim. 3:2*).
2. **Not double-tongued (v. 8):** Those who are double-tongued say one thing to certain people but then say something else to others or say one thing but mean another. They are two-faced and insincere. Their words cannot be trusted, so they lack credibility.
3. **Not addicted to much wine (v. 8):** A man is disqualified for the office of deacon if he is addicted to wine or other strong drink. Such a person lacks self-control and is undisciplined.
4. **Not greedy for dishonest gain (v. 8):** If a person is a lover of money, he is not qualified to be a deacon, especially since deacons often handle financial matters for the church.
5. **Sound in the faith and life (v. 9):** Paul also indicates that a deacon must "hold the mystery of the faith with a clear conscience." The phrase "the mystery of the faith" is simply one way Paul speaks of the Gospel. Consequently, this statement refers to the need for deacons to hold firm to the true Gospel without wavering. Yet this qualification does not merely involve one's beliefs, for he must also hold these beliefs "with a clear conscience." That is, the behavior of a deacon must be consistent with his beliefs.
6. **Blameless (v. 10):** Paul writes that deacons must "be tested first; then let them serve as deacons if they prove themselves blameless" (v. 10). "Blameless" is a general term referring to a person's overall character. Although Paul does not specify what type of testing is to take place, at a minimum, the candidate's personal background, reputation, and theological positions should be examined. Moreover, the congregation should not only examine a potential deacon's moral, spiritual, and doctrinal

maturity, but should also consider the person's track record of service in the church.
7. **Godly wife (v. 11):** According to Paul, deacons' wives must "be dignified, not slanderers, but sober-minded, faithful in all things" (v. 11). Like her husband, the wife must be dignified and respectable. Secondly, she must not be a slanderer or a person who goes around spreading gossip. A deacon's wife must also be sober-minded or temperate. That is, she must be able to make good judgments and must not be involved in things that might hinder such judgment. Finally, she must be "faithful in all things." This is a general requirement which functions similarly to the requirement for elders to be "above reproach" and for deacons to be "blameless."
8. **Husbands of one wife (v. 12):** The best interpretation of this difficult phrase is to understand it as referring to the faithfulness of a husband toward his wife. He must be a "one-woman man." That is, there must be no other woman in his life to whom he relates in an intimate way either emotionally or physically.
9. **Manage children and household well (v. 12):** A deacon must be the spiritual leader of his wife and children.[20]

Deacons Qualifications Expounded

When taking a closer look into the qualifications of a deacon, we see that Paul talks about:

"The Character of the Deacon" (1 Timothy 3:8a)

The Christian Standard Bible Commentary highlights the connection between Paul's list of elder/bishop/overseer/under-shepherd qualifications (1 Timothy 3:1–7), and his list of deacon qualifications. It says, "*Likewise* suggests a link between the lists of qualifications. There are striking similarities between the qualifications for pastor/overseer and for deacons. One key distinction is

---

20 Benjamin Merkle, "The Biblical Qualifications and Responsibilities of Deacons," *9 Mark Journal, Deacons* (March 2018).

The Seven

that deacons are not required to be able to teach."[21] Kenneth Barker and John Kohlenberger note that Paul wrote the deacons, like the overseers, are to be "worthy of respect." This word combines the ideas of gravity and dignity.[22]

"The Words of the Deacon" (1 Timothy 3:8b)

According to Max Anders and Knute Larson, the deacon is also to be sincere, literally "not double tongued." He must be known for truthfulness. His word must be reliable. His "yes" must be yes, and his "no," no (James 5:12).[23] J. Vernon McGee says this means that "a deacon should not be two-faced. A man's word should amount to something. It can be dangerous when a man tries to please everybody or doesn't have the courage to stand on his own two feet."[24]

"The Habits of the Deacon" (1 Timothy 3:8c)

The translation from The Apologetics Study Bible and the Christian Standard Bible is, "…not drinking a lot of wine…"[25] The Good News Translation says, "…they must not drink too much wine…"[26] This translation is to say that it is not the wine, but the excess of wine which is forbidden. The verb "(to be) given" at 3:8c is Strong's Number 4337, *prosecho*, which means "to be given, or addicted to; to attach one's self to; to hold or cleave to a person or a

---

21 *Christian Standard Bible* (Nashville, Tennessee: Holman Bible Publishers, 2017), 1922.
22 Kenneth Barker and John R Kohlenberger, *Zondervan NIV Bible Commentary* (Grand Rapids, Michigan: Zondervan Publishing House, 1994).
23 Knute Larson and Max Anders, *Holman New Testament Commentary: 1&2 Thessalonians, 1&2 Timothy, Titus, Philemon* (Nashville, Tennessee: B&H Publishing Group, 2000).
24 J Vernon McGee, *Thru the Bible Commentary Series: The Epistles: First and Second Timothy, Titus, Philemon* (Nashville, Tennessee: Thomas Nelson Publishers, 1991).
25 *Christian Standard Bible*, 1922.
26 Ibid.

thing.²⁷" So, the deacon, although not forbidden to drink altogether, is forbidden to allow the drink/wine to take control of him. He is forbidden to be given to it.

"The Desire of the Deacon" (1 Timothy 3:8d)

Paul always distanced himself from those who taught or preached for the sake of money. It is not surprising that he warned against deacons pursuing dishonest gain. Perhaps stories were still circulating about Judas pocketing the disciple's money for himself while presenting himself as a true follower of Jesus. Paul understood the lure of money, so he was careful in the area of finances, making certain that neither he nor the churches could be accused of greed or money-making schemes (1 Thessolonians 2:5; 2 Corinthians 8:20–21).²⁸ And maybe to press the import of knowing just how dangerous the handling of money could be, Paul would later advise Timothy that the love of money is the root of all evil: which while some coveted after, they have erred from the faith, and pierced themselves through with many sorrows (1 Timothy 6:10).

"The Sincerity of the Deacon" (1 Timothy 3:9)

John MacArthur says the word *mystery* describes truth previously hidden, but now revealed, including Christ's Incarnation, Christ's indwelling of Believers (Colossians 1:26–27), the unity of Jews and Gentiles in the church (Ephesians 3:4–6), the Gospel (Colossians 4:3), lawlessness (2 Thessalonians 2:7), and the rapture of the church (1 Corinthians 15:51–52).²⁹

"The faith," according to Barker and Kohlenberger, must be taken in an objective sense, referring to the truths of the Christian religion, rather than as subjective, having to do with one's personal

---

27 Biblehub, Strong's Exhaustive Concordance, accessed April 11, 2019, http://biblehub.com/greek/4337.htm.
28 Anders and Larson, *Holman New Testament Commentary*, 187.
29 John MacArthur, *The MacArthur Bible Commentary* (Nashville, Tennessee: Thomas Nelson, 2005).

faith in Christ. This letter has a strong emphasis on a pure "conscience" as well as a pure faith. A "clear conscience" is one that the blood of Christ has cleansed and does not offend God or other people.[30]

The Testing of the Deacon" (1 Timothy 3:10)

On this, Barker and Kohlenberger said, "This verb has three stages: (1) to test, (2) to prove by testing; and (3) to approve as the result of testing. Perhaps all three are in mind here. Before being accepted to serve as deacons, prospective deacons had to prove themselves beyond reproach before the community."[31] According to MacArthur, "the present tense of this verb (being found blameless) indicates an ongoing evaluation of deacons' character and service by the church." To be found blameless literally means "not able to be held" in a criminal sense; there is no valid accusation of wrongdoing that can be made against him.[32]

The Wife of the Deacon" (1 Timothy 3:11)

J. Vernon McGee defines this by saying that "grave" means they should be serious, able to be calm and cool. He says "not slanderers" means they are not to be gossips. A gossipy deacon's wife can cause much trouble in the church. "Sober," says McGee, is sober-minded. "Faithful in all things," he says, is for her to be faithful to her husband, to Christ Himself, and to His cause.[33]

---

30 Barker and Kohlenberger, *Zondervan NIV Bible Commentary*, 900.
31 Barker and Kohlenberger, *Zondervan NIV Bible Commentary*, 900.
32 MacArthur, *The MacArthur Bible Commentary*.
33 J Vernon McGee, *Thru the Bible Commentary Series: First and Second Timothy, Titus, Philemon* (Nashville, Tennessee: Thomas Nelson Publishers, 1991), 55.

"THE LIFESTYLE OF THE DEACON" (1 TIMOTHY 3:12)

On this, the Life Application Bible Commentary says, "This requirement matches the requirement for overseers spelled out in verses two, four-five, and is included for deacons for the same reasons."[34]

He should be a married man, the husband of one wife. This expression has been interpreted in several ways:

(1) He should not have more than one wife. This does not make sense because polygamy was rare in the cultures Paul visited, and it is never mentioned elsewhere as a problem in the early church.
(2) He should not be remarried after a divorce. Some scholars have argued strongly that this is the meaning Paul intended. Others have allowed that the Bible regards divorce as permissible in some conditions (Matthew 19:9; 1 Corinthians 7:15).
(3) He should not be remarried after his wife's death. Paul permitted remarriage for the widows (1 Timothy 5:14). He also refers to this in Romans 7:2–3, and 1 Corinthians 7:39.
(4) He should be faithful, not having mistresses or affairs. This view takes Paul's phrase to mean that the leader should be a one-woman man. This seems to be the best choice because the leader was to go against the immoral standards present in the pagan culture at Ephesus. The Bible rejects marriage as convenience and demands faithfulness and participation in the one flesh created by husband and wife (see Genesis 2:24; Ephesians 5:22–33).[35]

Barton, Veerman, and Wilson agree that the best interpretation of 1 Timothy 3:12 is that the deacon should be a one-woman man (after listing three other possible interpretations for the requirement).

---

34 Bruce Barton, David R Veerman, and Neil Wilson, *Life Application Bible Commentary 1&2 Timothy & Titus* (Wheaton, Illinois: Tyndale House Publishers, 1993), 69.

35 Barton, Veerman, and Wilson, *Life Application Bible Commentary 1&2 Timothy & Titus*, 69.

The Seven

This major point of scholarly debate deserves another look. With that look in mind, I see that regarding Paul's words of Ephesians 5:22–33, Marg Mowczko believes many Christians have missed Paul's highlighted point. Mowczko says that while many Christians believe that Paul used marriage to illustrate the close relationship between Jesus Christ and the church, it is actually the other way around: the unity between Christ and His church is a profound model for marriage. "As followers of Jesus," says Mowczko, "both husbands and wives should be building unity, nurture, love, and respect in their marriages."[36]

Located in the heart of the Household Codes to the Ephesians, Paul's words on marriage, Christ and the church avail themselves to a myriad of interpretations.[37] Ron Graham says that women do not have to submit to men in general, but only to their own men – their husbands in marriage. Graham says if a woman is going to put herself in subjection to a man, that man must be trustworthy as Christ is trustworthy to the church. But he (the husband) must be more than that. The husband must sacrifice himself and put his wife before himself in the spirit of Christ's sacrifice, according to Graham. The basis of a marriage is not a woman's submission to her husband. The basis is the husband's loving selflessness. He must make every necessary sacrifice for his wife's well-being. He cannot put his own personal interests first. His duty is to his wife, to his family, and to his household."[38] Barker and Kohlenberger simply said that the marriage tie takes precedence over every other human relationship and for this reason is to be regarded as inviolable.[39]

---

36 Marg Mowczko, Paul's Main Point in Ephesians 5:22-33, April 30, 2012, accessed April 22, 2019, http://margmowczko.com/pauls-main-point-in-eph-5_22-33/.

37 Oxford University Press, Household codes, accessed April 22, 2019, http://www.oxfordbiblicalstudies.com/article/opr/t94/e912.

38 Ron Graham, Husband and Wife: Ephesians 5:22-33, 2001, accessed April 22, 2019, http://www.simplybible.com/f74i-eph-husband-and-wife.htm.

39 Kenneth Barker and John Kohlenberger III, *NIV Commentary: Volume 2: New Testament* (Grand Rapids, Michigan: Zondervan Publishing House,

"The Testimony of the Deacon" (1 Timothy 3:13)

This all ties in because the deacon who is faithful to his wife in all things spiritual and physical, and who also serves well, will become known as a man who is to be trusted.[40] Those who serve well in their assigned duties in the church gain for themselves "an excellent standing." They should be able to maintain great respect in the eyes of the church as well as in God's sight.

Likewise, "great assurance" relates to confidence both before God and before other people.[41] This is the "boldness" in the faith, which is also in Christ Jesus. Remember that a deacon primarily has a spiritual office.[42]

THE SEVEN

Robert Naylor is one of several noted authors who wrote about infusing Acts 6:1–7 and 1 Timothy 3:8–13. To this end, many scholars simply refer to them as "The Seven." It is a matter of general agreement, however, that the election of these seven qualified men is the real beginning of the deacon as a church officer.[43]

Charles W. Deweese said that several key points emerge from the New Testament evidence concerning deacons. Although Bible scholars disagree over whether Acts 6:1–6 actually refers to deacons, virtually all agree that 1 Timothy 3:8–13 is a direct reference to them.[44] Robert Sheffield said that Acts 6:5 identifies seven men the early church chose to assist in the daily distribution of food to Grecian widows. Although Acts does not designate these men as deacons, their assignment "to wait on tables" (*Acts 6:2*) comes from the same root as the Greek word diakonos which can be translated

---

1994), 779.
40 McGee, *Thru the Bible Commentary*, 55.
41 Barker and Kohlenberger, *Zondervan NIV Bible Commentary*, 900.
42 McGee, *Thru the Bible Commentary*, 56.
43 Robert Naylor, *The Baptist Deacon* (Nashville, Tennessee: Broadman Press, 1955), 7.
44 Deweese, *The Emerging Role*, 11.

The Seven 31

into English as deacon or servant.[45] Howard B. Foshee took a more practical, holistic approach when he said that New Testament deacons have a noble heritage. Nevertheless, even more important they have a place of worthy purpose in both the present and the future, serving Christ as did "the seven" described in the Acts 6 account of the first church in Jerusalem. It is generally agreed that "deacon" soon evolved from the precedent set by "the seven."[46]

Moreover, that pattern did not evolve by happenstance. The author of the first printed letter to Timothy, the Apostle Paul, was allowed by God to have a bird's-eye view of exactly how the men he would describe as deacons ought to look and live. Before his Damascus Road experience, while he was still living in his days as Saul, Paul was making havoc of the church, entering every house, and dragging off men and women, committing them to prison. Paul was present when Stephen, the first-mentioned candidate being full of the Holy Spirit and wisdom, was stoned to death. Paul saw the mob stone Stephen, he saw and heard Stephen kneeling and calling on God before they stoned him saying, "Lord Jesus, receive my spirit and Lord, do not charge them with this sin." (Acts 7:59–60).

In full agreement with this murder, Paul was the one who held the coats of those who killed Stephen (Acts 7:58), so Paul knew how valuable deacons were to the church, and how important their lives and reputation meant to the church. Paul could tell Timothy about the kind of men the church would need because Paul saw it first-hand. He knew the power of the man in the role/ministry of deacon, and the fact that he helped to assassinate Stephen drove Paul into possibly being the perfect person to further the narrative of exactly how the deacon should look and live.

Acts 22:19–20 proves the effect of Steven's death on Paul. Even after God changed him, Paul was still apprehensive to go to the believers because he could not shake the memory of his past, saying,

---

45 Robert Sheffield, *Deacons as Leaders* (Nashville, Tennessee: Convention Press, 2016), 9.
46 Howard B. Foshee, *Now That You're a Deacon* (n.p.: Broadman Press, 1975), 12.

"'Lord, they know that in every synagogue I imprisoned and beat those who believe on You. And when the blood of Your martyr Stephen was shed, I also was standing by consenting to his death, and guarding the clothes of those who were killing him.'"[47]

Who better than Paul to bring the qualifications of the deacon to the forefront? With a past that caused him to hone in on the murder of Stephen with the microscope of his memory, Paul was now ready to focus on who and what the deacon should be.

Although Merkle brings this out with the flare of 21st century theology, this is not new theology at all. In 1688, Nehemiah Coxe, the son of the early Particular Baptist leader Benjamin Coxe, shared this on the advice from Paul to Timothy for the church:

> The rule of the church's proceeding in her election is laid before her, in an account of those qualifications which are requisite in persons to be employed in such a trust. They must be "men of honest report," men whose innocent and holy life is well-attested, persons of known and approved integrity, "full of the Holy Ghost and wisdom" (Acts 6:3). These general terms are comprehensive of the particulars mentioned by our apostle in that rule which he has given about the same matter in 1 Timothy 3:8-9. "Likewise, must the deacons be grave, not double-tongued, not given to much wine, not greedy of filthy lucre; holding the mystery of the faith in a pure conscience."
>
> It is an examination and trial of the persons to be chosen by this rule that the apostle intends in the next words, "And let these also first be proved [tested]; then let them use the office of [serve as] a deacon, being found blameless" (1 Timothy 3:10). This I mention [in order] that I may rectify a mistake which I think many have taken up from a misunderstanding of this text, wherein they suppose that the apostle requires that a trial should be made of elders and deacons in the discharge of the proper work of their office, before they are ordained to that office. But this way of trial is as foreign from the text, as the notion asserted is inconsistent with itself; for observe, he does

---

47 Darrell L. Bock, *ACTS Baker Exegetical Commentary on the New Testament* (Grand Rapids, Michigan: Baker Academic, 2007), 316.

not say: "Try whether they use the office of a deacon well" – which how can they do before they have it? – "and then let them be ordained, if for some time they have acquitted themselves well in it." But the trial he requires is antecedent to their using the office of a deacon and is no other than a diligent comparing of the qualification of the person with the characteristics of one meet for such an office that he had before set down.

This I take to be the plain sense of the words. And if this be not admitted, we must suppose the rule of one apostle to contradict the practice of others acting by the same infallible guidance as he wrote – which is absurd, for it is plain in Acts that they were directed to examine and look into the qualification and fitness of the persons to be chosen for deacons before they made choice of them, and that the apostles did by a solemn ordination vest them with their office before they acted in it, or used the office of a deacon.

As to the work of a deacon, the care of the poor is their special charge. And in order hereunto, the contributions and alms of the church are to be deposited with them, and entrusted to their distribution, as particular cases may require.[48]

Henry Webb has since summarized several centuries, decades, and years' worth of theological facts and debates concerning Paul's assertions of the deacon. Webb notes that the word *deacon* appears in our English Bible in only two passages. In Philippians 1:1, Paul greeted the church at Philippi and specifically greeted the overseers and the deacons. Paul gave the qualifications, first of the overseers and then of the deacons, in 1 Timothy 3. However, the word *diakonos*, which is translated "deacon" in those two Scripture passages, appears in that form and its related forms over one hundred times in the New Testament.[49] Usually it is translated either "servant" or "minister," "service" or "ministry," or "to serve" or "to minister." Only in these two passages did the translators choose not to trans-

---

48 Nehemiah Coxe, *Biblical Elders and Deacons* (Pensacola, Florida: Chapel Library, 2015), 8–9.
49 Henry Webb, *Deacons: Servant Models of the Church* (Nashville, Tennessee: Broadman and Holman, 2001).

late it but to create a new word. This was first done with the Latin translation as early as the fourth century.[50]

Since in both passages Paul used *diakonos* in association with the leadership role of the overseers (pastors), he seemed to be referring to a distinctive leadership role in the church. Thus, it seemed appropriate to transliterate *diakonos* (changing the i to an *e* and the *k* to a *c* and dropping the *os* ending), thereby creating a new word, *deacon*, rather than to use the general term *servant* or *minister*. Apparently as the number of Believers increased and new churches were begun, God led the congregations to formalize the servant role into a more specific church leadership role. The New Testament does not give a specific written job description for deacons. However, the job description is in the very name itself – deacons are to be servants. They are to be ministers working alongside the pastor/overseer.[51] Additionally, Webb admits that at times in church history, deacons have lost sight of their primary function of service.[52] In the book *The Emerging Role of Deacons*, Charles Deweese gives a thorough account of the changing understanding of deacon ministry through the centuries.

During the early centuries of the church's life, deacons understood their work to be primarily practical service. Their ministry included visiting the sick, administering the benevolence funds, providing pastoral care and preventive church discipline, assisting in the Lord's Supper and worship, and training new converts. Deacons in the Middle Ages from A. D. 500 to 1500 focused their work on worship. The primary reason the servant function of the deacon diminished during this period was that the role of deacon became the first stage toward the priesthood. Instead of the church roles being only distinctive in function, they became different levels or grades of ministry.[53] This shift in the focus of the deacon's role led to the sharp distinction between clergy and laity. One other factor

---

50   Webb, *Deacons: Servant Models of the Church*, 64.
51   Webb, *Deacons: Servant Models of the Church*, 64.
52   Ibid.
53   Ibid, 65.

in the loss of the deacon's ministry role was the rise of monastic orders that assumed responsibility for practical caring service. A restudy of the Reformers in the New Testament in the 16th century led to the rediscovery of the deacon as a servant. Both Martin Luther and John Calvin emphasized the deacon's role in distributing the church's aid to the poor.[54] Early Baptist deacons in England and America served as church officers. They were general servants of God, the church, and the needy. They assisted in limited administrative responsibilities.

A greater involvement in business functions began to emerge in the late 1700s and continued into the twentieth century. This business function involvement led to the concept of deacons as church business managers, acting as a board of directors. As a board of directors, deacons screened all major recommendations to determine whether they should go to the congregation. They controlled the finances, facilities, and other business affairs of the church. The pastor was directly responsible to the deacons rather than to the church.

This view of deacons as church business managers tended to distract from the other areas of service previously given strong attention. Statements such as these began to appear in church minutes and other writings: "Deacons, along with other church officers, are the chief managers of the church." "The duty of deacon is to take care of the secular concerns of a church." "The office of deacon is to relieve the minister from the secular concerns of the church." "A deacon's office extends only to the secular affairs of the church."[55]

In 1846, R. B. C. Howell published one of the most detailed books written on Baptist deacons up to that time. In this book *The Deaconship*, Howell identified the Twelve with the pastor and the Seven with the deacons. He designated deacons as the "financial officers of the church" and referred to them as "a board of officers, or the executive board of the church."[56] Based on his interpretation

---

54 Ibid.
55 Webb, *Deacons: Servant Models of the Church*, 65.
56 Ibid, 66.

of Acts 6, he assigned the temporal department of the church to the deacons and the spiritual department to the pastor. Howell's book was popular and has had a continuing influence on Baptist deacons. Howell's interpretation of Acts 6 and the role of deacons was continued by Prince E. Burroughs in his book *Honoring the Deaconship*. The Sunday School Board (now LifeWay Christian Resources) of the Southern Baptist Convention published this book and it was the official deacon study book from 1929 to 1956. Burroughs wrote, "As the apostles were forerunners of the pastors who later served the churches in a distinctly spiritual capacity, so these men [the Seven] were beyond doubt the forerunners of the deacons who later came to serve the churches in material affairs."[57]

Burroughs went on to say, "In the division of labor and the assignment of a place to the deacon, a fairly clear line was drawn as to the relation of the deacon to the church. On one side of the line stands the pastor. He is, shall we say, the ranking officer especially entrusted with the ministry, which is more distinctly spiritual. On the other side is the deacon, standing next to the pastor, and entrusted with the care of the material interests of the church. He is to care for the properties of the church, its buildings, its pastor's home, and its other material holdings. He is to direct and safeguard the financial side of its ministry."[58] Obviously, this book had a profound influence on the work of deacons in Baptist churches in the 20th century.

In the last half of the 1800s and through the 1900s, some church leaders questioned this limited scope of deacon ministry. These leaders cautioned against the misuse of authority by deacons and warned that the board concept violates Baptist church polity. The board approach may be appropriate for the business world but not for Baptist churches committed to congregational decision-making.

In *The Baptist Deacon*, released in 1955, Robert Naylor warned that among the deacons in many churches a certain "'bossism' has

---

57 Webb, *Deacons: Servant Models of the Church*, 66.
58 Ibid, 66.

developed. There is a 'board' complex and a general feeling that deacons are 'directors' of the church. Nothing could be further from the Baptist genius or the New Testament plan." However, Naylor continued to assume that deacons were business managers. Thus, he sent mixed signals to the deacons who read his book.[59]

An increasing number of church leaders frowned on the heavy involvement of deacons in church business and emphasized that deacons have spiritual duties. In the late 1950s and early 1960s Howard Foshee led in an intensive deacon study. The result was his book *The Ministry of the Deacon*, published in 1968, that had a profound influence in helping deacons rediscover their work as servants. Foshee not only reacted against the concept of deacons as a board of directors, but he also opposed the idea of deacons whose sole duties are the management of business matters. He wrote that deacons function in this limited way when they administer church affairs basically as a business operation, when their image is that of decision makers in all business affairs, and when business efficiency is a higher priority than Christian growth and service. In less than two decades, this book became a major factor in changing the deeply ingrained perception of deacons as business managers who run the church to a perception of deacons as ministers in partnership with the pastor.[60] Howell, Burroughs, and others misinterpreted Acts 6 and thus developed a wrong job description for deacons.[61] Dr. Young encapsulates all of that in a very personal, yet practical, way:

> One of the things I say (to men that I am training to be deacons), from what I have been able to gather from study and everything else is that *diakonos*, basically translates two different words – *dia*, which is 'through,' and *konos*, which is 'dust,' which literally means that word deacon comes from, as best we understand, a person who had a servant and called that servant and the servant came running through the dust to serve. And so, to be a deacon, literally, in terms of the concept,

---

59 Webb, *Deacons: Servant Models of the Church*, 67.
60 Ibid.
61 Ibid, 68.

is to be so willing and ready to serve until you come running and kick up dust as you come, because you want to serve. And so, what I have done is try to explain to them that the biblical concept of deacon is servant, and that Pastor Howell, who was in Nashville, Tennessee, who translated that word as 'Board,' mistranslated the word, and people took that to mean, 'We're the Board.' That is not what it is. It is, 'Over this ministry.' So, the deacons are involved in ministry. So, what we've tried to do is, get people to understand here at our church, over training; over a period of time, is that, literally, deacons are partners with the pastor in ministry. That's the biblical concept – that we serve. (And) That the deacon's greatest role is to serve. In fact, we talk, essentially, from studying and gathering from all – everywhere – we've concluded that the concept is very simple. Deacons came into the church because there was a need for people to serve. And so, we say that the deacon's primary role is to serve God, to serve the people, and to serve with the pastor. Bottom line; that's (the) biblical concept.[62]

Coming from the Apostle Paul, the men Paul described to Timothy are the kind of men who understand this concept, and literally live to carry it out.

Platt, Akin, and Merida say, "When we consider 1 Timothy 3:8–13, along with our discussion of Acts 6, we can see two main qualifications for deacons. First, they must have a mission mindset. The church was growing in the early chapters of Acts at a breathtaking speed, and the church needed leaders who would embrace the mission God had given them and unite others in the same cause. This is the reason why deacons cannot be small-minded individuals engrossed in turf wars, maintaining their rights and lobbying for their own causes. Instead, they are to see the mission of the church and work to help others understand that mission. Every facet of their ministry is part of that overarching mission.

"The church is on a mission to make the Gospel known in all nations, which is exactly why the adversary delights in turning the church of Jesus Church inward on itself at every opportunity.

---

62 Personal Interview, "Jerry Young," September 2018.

Satan loves seeing the church embroiled in battles over this or that issue. In such cases deacons may be called in to absorb the shock. Certainly, valid complaints and real needs arise, and when they do, deacons should rise to meet those needs so the mission of the church can thrive. Churches can get so engrossed in catering to every complaint that the primary mission of the church gets lost. Therefore, if someone is pulling the church away from its mission, that person is not qualified to be a deacon. This leads to the second qualification.

"Deacons must have a Christlike character. Scripture doesn't give us a lot of detail regarding what deacons do, but it does make the character of deacons pretty clear. We might say Scripture is more concerned about the sanctity of our lives than the structure of our leadership."[63]

> *Tremble, Sir Deacon, tremble, church member, if you are not what you confess to be; there is a doom awaiting you of a fiercer, a direr sort than even for the ungodly and the reprobate. From the height of your profession you shall be plucked down. You have built your nest among the stars, but you must make your bed in hell.* – C. H. Spurgeon[64]

---

[63] David Platt, Daniel L. Akin, and Tony Merida, *Christ-centered Exposition: Exalting Jesus in 1&2 Timothy and Titus* (Nashville, Tennessee: B&H Publishing Group, 2013).

[64] Kerry James Allen, *Spurgeon's Quotes: The Definitive Collection* (The Woodland, Texas: Kress Biblical Resources, 2018), M–512.

CHAPTER THREE
THE PLAN IN THE EXPERIENCE OF THE AFRICAN-AMERICAN CHURCH

During one of the opportunities to teach a deacon's class in our association's annual Congress of Christian Education, I asked the question: "What did God have in mind when He appointed the office of deacon to His church? In other words, what is the most important duty of the deacon?" Before the question could be repeated, a hand was raised quickly and excitedly, and I cautiously acknowledged the hand. "Yes, sir…what is the most important duty of the deacon? What is the most important thing that the deacon must do above everything else? What did God have in mind when He blessed the church with deacons?" The student yelled his answer: "Lead the devotion!"

If you had been there, you probably would have thought the earth moved. If not the earth, at least you would have felt the room shake.

On all that is holy, if I had been sitting down, the chair would not have been able to hold me. To say that disbelief covered my face is an absolute understatement. The student continued:

"The most important thing a deacon can do is to lead the devotion! That's it! There is nothing else more important than that! Everybody knows that!"

He was so sure of his answer. He answered with confidence and pride. However, I had to correct him. I just was not ready for the response after the correction.

"Sir," I responded, "Do you really think that when God blessed the church with the office of the deacon, that God had devotion in mind? Do you really believe that? Think about this long and hard. Do you really believe that?"

"Yes, I do, because that's the number one thing that the deacon has to do! That's number one on the list. Every Sunday, before he does anything else, he has to lead that devotion! He has to get the church ready!"

I began to plead with the student: "But, sir, we have just had an introduction into Acts 6 and you have seen where deacons come from and why. Do you still really believe that what we call devotion is the number one thing that God would have the deacons to do? Please listen to me carefully."

Again, I begged the student and repeated the question – very slowly – to make sure that the student understood exactly what was being asked. The entire back-and-forth began to take on a one-on-one feel.

"When God gave the ministry of deacons to the church, do you really, really believe that He had the devotion period in mind? Do you really believe that God expects the deacon to care more about singing a song, lining and then singing a hymn, reading Scripture, praying, and then singing another song (standing in front of the congregation for about 15 minutes), more than He expects anything else out of the deacons' ministry? Think about that, now. Do you really, really believe that?" (Lining a hymn means a deacon would outline the selected hymn in a talking voice, then the congregation would repeat what has just been outlined in a singing voice. This is done in a call-and-response type of manner).

"Yes – I – do!" was the emphatic reply. It almost came off the student's tongue in a defiant manner. The deliberate reply had a ring to it as if to say, "Nobody can change my mind on this. I know what I am talking about."

"Sir, where did you get that from? Who told you this? Who taught this to you?" was my next rebuttal/question.

The reply of the student: "My pastor! My pastor taught me this! He told me this a long time ago!"

As the student's last reply grew in decibels and intensity, the fact that the other students in the class agreed with the answering student had a deep effect upon me. I even heard a spattering of, "That's right. That's right." echoing throughout the classroom. More than a few students agreed that the beginning of the Sunday morning worship service, often started by as few as two and sometimes up to as many as ten deacons, was the reason why God gave deacons to the church.

This entire dialogue, between the outspoken student and the silent, yet agreeing, students with the instructor, serves as a microcosm of what I feared was the case all along. Down through the history of the Black Church, the deacon's assumed role of worship leader has blinded the deacon of his true Biblical assignment. To the blinded deacon, if he does not lead devotion, then he is not a deacon at all. To him, everything hinges on the devotion.

In his book, *The Deacon in the Black Baptist Church*, Dr. T. DeWitt Smith, Jr., the current pastor of Trinity Baptist Church of Metro Atlanta, says that in churches where the pastor has no pulpit assistants to serve during worship, the deacons quite frequently participate as worship leaders. They read Scripture, pray and lead the church in a most reverent state of mind. Smith says that in many of our congregations, the practice of having the deacons lead the devotional service before the processional of the choir is still very common. In some congregations, the deacons lead a devotional service that begins after the call to worship and the processional. In some congregations, the deacons do not have any part of a devotional service until the weekly prayer service. The pastor usually decides as the Holy Spirit leads.[65]

---

65 T. DeWitt Smith Jr., *The Deacon in the Black Baptist Church* (Atlanta, Georgia: Hope Publishing House, 1992), 61.

For the congregations of the First West Florida Baptist District Association, the devotion service usually follows this format: one deacon will open up with a welcome/greeting and a congregational song, and another deacon will then read Scripture. After the Scripture, a deacon will line the hymn that the deacons and the congregation sing together. A different deacon will then lead the prayer that follows, if the number of deacons available permits. If the number of deacons does not permit different leaders, the same deacon will line the hymn and pray.

Following the prayer, the deacon who led the congregational song will sing a closing song. The deacon who gave the original greeting will follow that song in closing the devotion with a hearty, "Come on and get involved in the service," type of phrase. This is the variation of "devotion" in the African American church of the First West Florida Baptist District Association.

Knowing all of this, upon my engaging with the student and hearing the student's passionate – although uninformed – reply, my heart was broken. But my eyes were opened. The argument was not worth a fight, but I proceeded to teach that the position of the student about deacons held absolutely no Biblical explanation to lead the worship service. I drilled home that the pastor, as the God-appointed, spiritual leader of God's people, is the de facto leader of every ministry of the congregation, including the role of the primary worship leader. The pastor may or may not employ others to fill that role. If he does employ others to lead worship, that employment does not ever abdicate him from the responsibility of being the worship leader. The pastor, with the Holy Spirit leading him, oversees the entire Sunday morning worship program and the deacon has no inherent role in that provision. With God leading the pastor to do so, the pastor can alter or totally subtract the devotion period from the Sunday morning docket in favor of whatever form of worship to which the Lord leads.

The student with the quick answer was aspiring to become a deacon at his church. His pastor, the instructor later found out, sent the aspiring deacon to the class for training. A total of six men came to the class from that congregation. That aspiring deacon, however, did not finish the week in the deacon class. In addition, I was not invited back to teach the class the following year. When I asked the pastor of the aspiring deacon about the comment and the teaching the gentleman had received prior to his coming to the class, the pastor was dumbfounded and at a total loss for words. So was I.

The reality is stark with devotion being held in such a high regard in the Black Baptist church. Still, it certainly bears repeating that this is nothing new. Devotion has long been the very start of the worship experience in church on Sunday morning. Holistically speaking, worship should be a spiritual experience that helps the Believers enjoy the presence of the Lord. Deacons do play a great role in the corporate worship service of the church; however, they are there to inspire people to worship. How the deacons act and react to the singing, prayers, Scripture readings, sermon, offering and call to discipleship often determines how that congregation will act and react. According to DeWitt, "If the deacons come to church on fire, the church will catch fire and be a torchlight to the community at large.[66]

Much to the personal and theological chagrin of the research for this project, it must be conceded that many Baptist congregations do have expectations of how deacons should participate in the worship services of the church. In some churches, deacons are expected to lead or share in a devotional period of 10-15 minutes before the regularly scheduled worship services begin. This might include Scripture and leading in prayer and congregational singing. Usually deacons' leadership in worship is not limited to Sunday morning services. The same is often expected during seasonal revivals, midweek services and the occasional Sunday afternoon program that still occurs in many Black Baptist churches. This would extend to those occasions when more than one congregation worships together, whether that is to mark a liturgical holiday, to honor a

---

66 T. DeWitt Smith Jr., *The Deacon in the Black Baptist Church* (Atlanta, Georgia: Hope Publishing House, 1992), 61.

board or ministry of the church, or to celebrate a church or pastoral anniversary.[67]

The African American church views the devotion time with the expectation that the deacon has a level of power within the church. Being dumbfounded, therefore, is the expected norm of those of us who may not see the traditional role of deacon, for example leading the devotion time, as valid.

The aspiring deacon in that class tried to explain that the deacon was the leader of the church because he, himself, was a leader in his job and a leader in the congregation. Therefore, he believed, the deacon had the power and responsibility to lead the devotion time, lead the pastor, lead the congregation and lead any/everything else in the church. This is the reality but, according to Dr. Young, it is not a new or isolated reality.

> At New Hope, the deacons and I are partners. I mean, I have the best relationship with the deacons at our church than I do with anybody. Period. I mean, we are literally partners in ministry. We serve effectively together. That is, in my mind, the biblical model; that's what the Bible actually envisions. However, this is the exception as opposed to the rule. As president of the National Baptist Convention, many of the calls I get asking for help – I get those calls from pastors who are having difficulty with their deacons. I mean, it happens over and over again. And when you get involved in it and you try to ascertain what has happened, you discover that there is an unbiblical concept of what it means to be a deacon and that the secular has invaded the sacred. As a result they are taking their marching orders from the secular as opposed to what ought to be happening in the sacred. And that is the bottom line. If the Baptist church is going to not just survive, but thrive, [then] we are going to have to change the paradigm as it relates to pastors and deacons – away from the secular to more of the sacred.[68]

---

67 Marvin A. McMickle, *Deacons in Today's Black Baptist Church* (Valley Forge, Pennsylvania: Judson Press, 2010).
68 Dr. Jerry Young, interview by Lonnie Wesley, September 27, 2018.

The overwhelming majority of the African American church is, indeed, Baptist. Because the National Baptist Convention is the largest African American organization with approximately 7.5 million members, Dr. Young receives many requests to assist congregations in the convention with misunderstandings concerning deacons.[69]

This is a reality. Within the African American Baptist church, this is a very strong reality; although, it is not solely limited to the NBCUSA. Dr. Fred Luter, the former president of the Southern Baptist Convention, gives his perception of the reality from the Southern Baptist perspective. The Southern Baptist Convention (SBC) is a fellowship of over 47,000 Baptist churches scattered across the United States and its territories. The convention has more than 39,000 Anglo congregations, 3,228 African-American congregations, 2,103 Hispanic congregations, 734 Korean congregations, and 399 Native American congregations.[70]

> Unfortunately, what I've seen across the country in a lot of the churches is that there is always this tension, this power struggle (for the lack of a better word) between the deacons and the pastors. And it just should not be. If all of us understand our role, because right before – in Timothy – where he gives the qualification of the deacon, he gives the qualifications of the preacher, right before. Both of us are given qualifications by God that we should meet as pastors and deacons. And the bottom line is when we cross that line, that is when the tension happens. That's when the competition happens. There should be no competition between a pastor and a deacon. Deacons should be there to serve the pastors. Pastors should be there to teach and train and be an example for the deacons. But we've messed this up so much through the years in churches. And I've seen this in White and Black churches where, unfortunately, we've usurped each other's authority and now it becomes a popularity

---

[69] Meg Anderson, National Baptist Convention, USA, Inc. (1895--), 2017, accessed January 21, 2019, http://www.blackpast.org/aah/national-baptist-convention-usa-inc-1895.

[70] Fast Facts About the Southern Baptist Convention, 2017, accessed January 21, 2019, http://www.sbc.net/fastfacts/.

contest of who can we get (for the membership) to support our point of view. I heard George McCalep say years ago that the (Deacon) Board mentality has given a lot of deacons the big-head like the buck stops with us. Here (at Franklin Avenue Baptist Church), we changed the name from Deacon Board to Deacon Ministry, because they are to minister to the people. But we need to change that mentality from Deacon Board to Deacon Ministry because that word "board" has given many of them the perception that "I'm ruling. The buck stops with us."[71]

Along with Young and Luter, Smith describes the spirit of the aspiring deacon further, which explains yet another reality of the African American Baptist church. Smith says one of the strongest misconceptions about the job of the deacon is the amount of influence and power that he (the deacon) has. The contention and strife that grows from such erroneous thinking has its roots in the fact that the deacon of yesteryear was often the boss of the church. He gave the orders. His board was the "powers that be." If someone wanted anything, including the pastor, he had to get the pre-approval and permission of the deacon body. The chief problem that resulted in the Black Church was that the deacon brother saw himself as the church's overlord and not as a spiritual under-shepherd. It is a serious indictment against the churches of years past that they put powerful men in office to serve as deacons instead of men with Spirit-power who saw it as their distinct privilege to serve the church. The problem has extended itself to these modern times in which we now live.[72]

Within a survey of congregations of the First West Florida Baptist District Association, of whom all are members of the NBCUSA, Inc., when asked if the deacon ministry "oversees the pastor," and if "the pastor was accountable to the deacons," 31 percent of those responding answered in the affirmative in one or both of those

---

71 Personal Interview, "Dr. Fred Luter," September 2018.
72 T. DeWitt Smith, *The Deacon in the Black Baptist Church* (Atlanta, Georgia: Hope Publishing House, 1992), 11.

The Seven 49

areas.[73] A third of the congregants (survey responders) had the mindset that the deacon stands in the role of pastoral and ministerial overseer instead of being in the role of a servant. That perception may speak to the even longer-lasting consternation between pastors and deacons, and deacons and the church.

Dr. Marvin McMickle, the pastor of Antioch Baptist Church in Cleveland, Ohio and the author of *Deacons in Today's Black Baptist Church*, cements the findings of the survey and the respondents' answers when he says that perhaps more than any other concern related to the office of the deacon that generates the most tension and controversy is the relationship between the Black Baptist pastor and the board of deacons. Baptist churches in the United States have been debating about this relationship for at least two hundred years, and nowhere is that debate and division more prevalent than in our Black churches. At the heart of the debate is a single question: Is the deacon's job to oversee and regulate the ministry of the pastor, or is the deacon's job to serve the needs of the people in support of the pastor?[74] Dr. Luter said:

> Again, if we are looking at it from a Biblical point of view, in the book of Acts the congregation-deacon relationship should be that the deacons are there to serve. They visit the sick. They give out communion. They lead in prayer. They are basically there to serve the local congregation. Anything other than that, I think they are getting outside of their assigned Biblical role. And that's the problem in many of our churches. They've gotten outside of their Biblical roles and they're not doing the things that the Bible said. They are doing things totally different. And a lot of that has to do with that Deacon Board mentality. It has messed a lot of us (a lot of our churches) up.[75]

The reality of the deacon not knowing/understanding whether he is a leader or a servant in the church, or not understanding how

---

73 Wesley, Lonnie "First West Florida Baptist District Association Survey," November18-29, 2018.
74 McMickle, *Deacons in Today's Black*, 48.
75 Dr. Fred Luter, interview by Lonnie Wesley, September 27, 2018.

to lead by serving in the church, may be another leading problem. And another strong challenger to this top-ranking reality that must be faced in the Black Church is the reality of how, or if the deacon is trained before he becomes a deacon. If some sort of training should occur, exactly how should that be done? And by whom? And when?

When asked of the emphases when training deacons, Dr. Luter gladly obliged:

> I think the first thing that should be emphasized most is your servant position – that's the first thing. Deacons are servants. You are here to serve the people. Secondly, we have to emphasize accountability. You are accountable to the pastor and to the church. And then, thirdly, your faithfulness. You are a deacon. That means that you're a leader. You need to be here for worship. You need to be here for Bible Study. You need to be here for Sunday School. You need to be an example in tithes, in offering, in conduct. All of these things involve the proper role of deacons. And this comes from if the membership requires certain things of the pastor, then I think we should require certain things of the deacon. And so, what we emphasize here (at Franklin Street Baptist Church), and what I think the Bible emphasizes, when we look at the role of deacons, their number one priority is being a servant.[76]

Dr. Luter's assessment rings true, the deacon is a servant. I also agrees with Smith when Smith says that training is essential for the deacon who is privileged to serve in the Black Baptist church. We have let ignorance and the need for money rule us long enough. We should extend our scope of Christian education and development for service to the deacons of our churches. Train them to know their job so well that they can be trusted to instruct others, which is a function of discipling. A trained diaconate will be a credit to any church group and pastor who, in turn, will thank the Lord.[77]

---

76 Personal Interview, "Dr. Fred Luter", September 2018).
77 T. DeWitt Smith Jr., *The Deacon in the Black Baptist Church* (Atlanta, Georgia: Hope Publishing House, 1992), 44-45.

With each congregation carrying her appropriate status of autonomy, the congregations of the Black Baptist church do not share a prescribed program of study to train their deacons. The decision of training is usually left up for the pastor to do or not do. The same is said for whether the deacon is ordained or installed into the deacon ministry.

McMickle says that the Jerusalem church selected the seven individuals named in Acts 6:1–7, and they were consecrated immediately, and the apostles set them to work. In contrast, he says, in the Black Baptist church of the twenty-first century, it is considered desirable that persons chosen to be deacons should go through a carefully designed period of training before they begin their term of service. That training period typically lasts for one year, and during that time the candidates for the position of deacons are known as "trial deacons" or "walking deacons." This twelve-month time frame is a probationary period during which two important things occur. First, the church observes the candidates to see how seriously they are taking their new duties. For example, are the trial deacons regular in their church attendance and are they faithful in carrying out any and all duties assigned to them during this time? Second, the trial deacons can determine whether or not serving as a deacon for a full term, which in the Black Baptist church is more than likely to be a life term, is something they really want to do. Those trial deacons who complete the training period are then accepted for ordination, or for whatever installation service the local church deems appropriate.[78]

It is the level of what is appropriate, which is in the eye of the beholder, that seems to be the genesis of whether a church reaches a certain level of Biblical understanding concerning deacons. What is good for one congregation may not be so good for another congregation. Dr. Young gives us his point of view:

> Well, here again…at New Hope…I will use our church. I've said this to pastors when I was the president of the state convention of Mississippi. And, a lot of the guys said, "Well,

---

78 McMickle, *Deacons in Today's Black*, 56.

I've had so many problems with deacons until, what I'm going to do, I'm going to appoint the deacon so that I can disappoint him. I'm going to appoint him and then I can disappoint him." And I said to them, "Well, that's not my approach. Here is my approach. My approach is to literally ordain deacons. I ordain into ministry." And I said, "Let me tell you how I do it." We provide the congregation with nomination forms so that the congregation will nominate people they believe ought to be involved in the deacon ministry. Once those nomination forms are collected, I have a group of deacons who will go through those nomination forms, through a screening process. Then they interview the perspective deacons and then they finally come to me and say, "Brother Pastor, out of the list of 35 men, we believe 20 of those men have great potential to become deacons in our church, and here's the reason why the other 15…we don't believe they qualify; we don't believe they make it. And out of the 20, there's five of those, we believe, they need to come and see you. And these are the five that we believe." And once that's done, we go back and we say, "Okay, these are the 20 people, then, that we believe ought to be trained." They are trained. The training used to be a whole year. The deacons said, "Pastor, they thought we were slow." So, the training is not a year anymore. Every deacon has got to come to training. And the training usually lasts for about four months; every week. We have weekly sessions and it's about four months. Sometimes it ends up being five (months). But that's how we do it, in terms of extensive training. And these are the people that the church has recommended. Once those persons have completed the training; these are the men that you have nominated. These are the men that now we are saying we want to ordain to ministry and the church validates it, and then we have an ordination service where the church is involved in that process.

And the reason it's an ordination thing and the church is involved in that whole process, because what we do is, once they've been trained, during the ordination we have men to get up and tell the church what the training has meant to them. What the training did for them. What they understand about being a deacon. What the purpose is of deacons in the church. What their relationship is. All of that is a part of the ordination service. So that, not only does the deacon now get trained as to what he should or should not be doing, but the church understands it as well. So, the church has a much greater appreciation now for that relationship.[79]

This reality is a strength of the Black Church and overwhelmingly so because it stretches outside the bounds of race. If this is a universal church problem, then this project and the comments from Dr. Traylor are a necessity for the body of Christ. Notice Dr. Traylor's additional comments:

> Well, we've got to get back to waiting tables and serving. And they are (the men of Acts 6) preaching the gospel and sharing and meeting the needs of the church and, goodness, that's what the deacon has got to do.[80]

Regardless of his race.

---

79 Personal interview, "Jerry Young," September 2018.
80 Personal Interview, "Dr. Ted Traylor," September 2018.

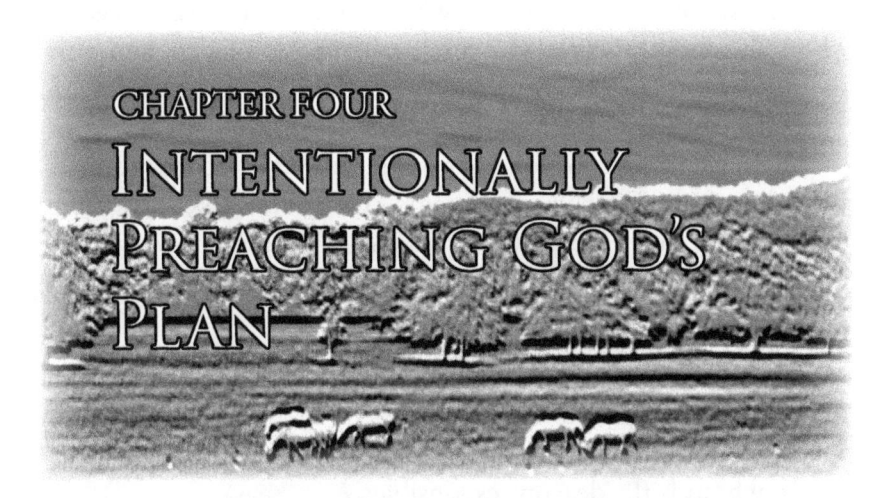

CHAPTER FOUR
INTENTIONALLY PREACHING GOD'S PLAN

To properly address the present realities of devotion being an absolute necessity of the deacon, of the presumed power of the deacon, of the misunderstood role of the deacon, of the training (or lack thereof) of the deacon, and of the overall qualifications of the deacon, the gospel is the only hope. Minds cannot be changed but for the gospel. As the Apostle Paul admonished the Romans, he also admonishes us not to be conformed to the world, but to be transformed by the renewal of our minds. Paul tells us that we may discern what is the good, acceptable or perfect will of God.

God used Paul as the vessel to give the qualifications of deacons to Timothy. Paul also stressed the importance of the gospel of our Lord and Savior, Jesus. The gospel was important to Paul, and he wanted it to be important to others. Paul taught that the gospel was important because God planned it, because of the person at its center, and because of its purpose.[81] In short, the Gospel is important because of its plan, its person, and its purpose.

To that end, and during the preparation for this work, I preached four (4) expository sermons to the congregants of Greater Little Rock. All four sermons shared the subject matter of the office

---

81 Jay Taylor, Why the Gospel is Important: Galatians 1, February 2008, accessed February 23, 2019, http://www.bible.ca/ef/expository-galatians.

of deacons. Among other items, these sermons addressed who the deacon is, what the deacon is, when the deacon was/is needed, where the deacon is needed, why the deacon is needed, and how the deacon came to be. The Biblical qualifications of the deacon were also covered in the four sermons.

Before and after the four-sermon series was preached, a survey was administered to the congregants. The survey asked the same questions to both the 8:00am and the 10:45am crowds of the Greater Little Rock congregation. Here are the questions:

1. What is the primary responsibility of the deacon?
2. Whom do deacons serve in the church?
3. Name one responsibility of the deacon?
4. To whom is the pastor responsible?
5. To whom is the deacon responsible?
6. YES or NO…the deacon runs the church?
7. YES or NO…the deacon oversees the pastor?
8. YES or NO…with the changing of times, is the office of deacon outdated and not needed for the church today?
9. How would you describe the pastor-deacon relationship at your church?
10. How has a deacon been influential in your personal and/or church life?[82]

After this survey was given before the sermon on week one, the following sermons were preached:

SERMON #1

Sermon #1 was preached on October 7, 2018. The title of the sermon was, **"The Results of Helping the Pastor."** The text was Acts 6:1–7. I told the congregation of when I first read *The Church Afire*, by R. Kent Hughes. I told the church of how Dr. Hughes took on the Book of Acts in a very detailed way. Chapter two of this work is the detailed account of how Dr. Hughes handled the text of Acts 6:1–7, and that particular reference served this sermon well.

---

[82] Deacon Survey, Appendix A

Acts 6 shows us Satan trying to disrupt the inward peace of the early church. Wonderful things were happening as the new church grew by leaps and bounds. Three thousand received Christ at Pentecost. Another 2,000 were added shortly thereafter. Acts 5 tells us that many more were then added to the church. Satan, unhappy about God's success, sowed a spirit of murmuring and a seed of gossip among God's people, hoping to set believer against believer.

Countless works for God have been destroyed in this way.[83] To uplift the people of God, the Spirit led to giving a word of cautious expectation when it comes to ministry, more specifically, in helping the pastor. Therefore, this text and sermon were both used to point out what happens when someone steps forward to help the pastor in the ministry. To press the main thought of the message, the following question was asked: "What happens when someone steps forward to help the pastor? Leaning heavily on verse seven of the text, it was submitted to God's people that the result of answering the call to help the pastor is that:

1) THE WORD GROWS (verse seven, "A")
2) THE CHURCH GROWS (verse seven, "B")
3) THE LEADERS GROW (verse seven, "C")

Sermon #2

Sermon #2 was preached on October 14, 2018. The title of the sermon was, **"What the Deacon – and Everybody – Should Know."** The text was Acts 6:8–15; 7:54–60.

In this message, verse eight is the highlighted verse because verse eight turns the subject matter around to a more dramatic scene. Since Sermon #2 followed Sermon #1 in a series-preaching style, the reference to the former, immediate Scripture was easy to follow.

The Holy Spirit showed the pastor the plan, and the question was then asked: "What should the deacon (and everybody) know?" Using the verses of Acts 7:1 to Acts 7:53 as a background, the congregants were told that:

---

83 R. Kent Hughes, *ACTS- The Church Afire* (Wheaton, Illinois: Crossway Books, 1996), 93.

1) The deacon should KNOW THE WORD OF GOD (beginning at 7:2)
2) The deacon should KNOW WHERE TO LOOK (verses 55–56)
3) The deacon should KNOW WHAT TO SAY (verses 59–60)

At Acts 7:2, Stephen is spreading the Word of God. This preacher is not one of those preachers who say that deacons are preachers. On the contrary, this preacher is one of those Christians who believes that ALL Christians should know the Word of God! And you do not have to be a preacher to know the Word. You do not have to be a preacher to proclaim the Word. You do not have to be a preacher to spread the Word. All of God's children should know the Word. Stephen knew the Word well enough to tell his listeners about Abraham and about Joseph and about Moses. He told them about Joshua and about David. Stephen knew the Word.

Not only that, but Luke also shows us in verses 55–56 that when Stephen was in trouble, Stephen also knew where to look. Where did he look? When Stephen was in trouble, he gazed up into heaven, and he saw the glory of God and Jesus standing at the right hand of God. And then Stephen said, "Behold, I see the heavens opened, and the Son of Man standing at the right hand of God."

Lastly, Stephen shows us that he knew what to say. We see this in verses 59–60. As they were stoning him, Stephen cried out, "Lord Jesus, receive my spirit." And falling to his knees, he cried out with a loud voice, "Lord, do not hold this sin against them." When he had said this, he fell asleep.

This point was made to remind the listening congregation that the chosen men of Acts 6 were not called "deacons," per se, but they certainly can be looked to as being the forerunner of those who currently hold the office of deacon. A more important part of that is the fact that Stephen was striving to be like Christ, as all Christians should be. Stephen knew who his enemies were, but he did not wish them ill. Instead, Stephen prayed that they would be forgiven just like His Savior prayed when He was on Calvary's cross. Stephen knew the Word, he knew where to look, and he knew what to say.

SERMON #3

Sermon #3 was preached on October 21, 2018. The title of the sermon was, "**Thank God for the Deacon.**" The text was 1 Timothy 3:8–13.

In this message, the position, the potential, and the person of the deacon were each elevated. The ever-popular down-talking and joking about the deacon was discouraged, and the upholding of the deacon was encouraged.

A part of the conversation between the pastor and Dr. Jerry Young (President of the National Baptist Convention, USA) was shared with the congregation in order to enlighten them. It was communicated that the Greek word for deacon breaks down into "*dia*," which means "through," and "*konos*," which means "the dust." So, *diakonos* shows us that the deacon is one who literally runs so fast to serve that he kicks up dust on his way. It was said that the deacon wants to have the opportunity to serve or help somebody so badly that you can see dust kick up from his heels as he runs! Soon after that breakdown, the following statement was made:

> And I think that is where all the lines get crossed up. I think that is the onus of the communication problem between church and deacon, between people and deacon, or between community and deacon. You see, traditionally, because the pew has not correctly understood what it means to be a deacon, the deacon has thusly been expected by the people to do some things that God has never expected him to do! Traditionally, most of us know that the people have expected the deacon to be the leader, when that is not what the Lord has expected him to be. The Lord has expected him to be a servant! Most congregations have not been fair to the office of deacon because they have asked the deacon to lead when the Lord has instructed him to follow!

An expository look into what Paul told Timothy about the office of deacon, and how Paul described the deacon to Timothy, was then shared with the congregation. Pastor Mark Dever, the longtime pastor of Capitol Hill Baptist Church in Washington, D. C., and the founder of 9 Marks Ministries, was mentioned. One of the writers of Dr. Dever's blog said the deacon is both a shock absorber and a servant.[84]

The deacon is a shock-absorber because (according to the teachings of Acts 6), the forerunners to the office of deacons literally stepped in and took the shock. These guys absorbed whatever would have otherwise fallen on the apostles. These seven did the work in the middle of the congregation, keeping it off the pastor, which allowed the pastor to keep his mind on the preaching of the Word. He is a shock-absorber.

He is also a servant. The deacon serves. That is what he does. The deacon does not look to be served, but to serve. That is why the preacher said he thanks God for the deacon.

SERMON #4

Sermon #4 was preached on December 2, 2018. It was a sermon of cautious encouragement. The title of the sermon was **"When Serving Meets Persecution."** The text was Acts 8:1–8.

In delivering this sermon, the very first thing the preacher was blessed to do was quote the rich, timeless masterpiece, *The Cost of Discipleship,* where that great German theologian Dietrich Bonhoeffer said, "When Christ calls a man, he bids him come and die."[85] After this quote, the preacher then declared, "That, my friends, sums up Acts 7, and it bridges all the way to Acts 8 for us today."

The pastor pressed the fact that persecution is a necessary part of following Christ. If you follow Him, you will be persecuted,

---

84 Jamie Dunlop, Deacons:Shock-Absorbers and Servants, March 31, 2010, accessed April 11, 2019, http://www.9marks.org/article/deacons-shock-absorbers-and-servants/.

85 Dietrich Bonhoeffer, *The Cost of Discipleship* (New York, New York: Touchstone, 1959), 89.

The Seven 61

and you will be wronged. You will be mistreated, and you will be victimized. If you follow Christ, you will be offended, and you will be injured. Your feelings will be hurt. You will be insulted. There will be times when you will get upset. You will be snubbed. When you dare to give God glory, when you dare to give Him the praise, when you have the courage to stand up for Jesus, or when you have the nerve/guts to worship and serve Him, you will be persecuted!

The question was asked: "What happens when serving meets persecution?" The following are the answers that were given:
1) Persecution (more of it) (verse one)
2) Pandemonium (verse three)
    a. Perfidious pandemonium (Paul *made* havoc…)
    b. Prophetic pandemonium (verses four and five, in light of verse eight)
3) Pleasure (verse eight)

When serving meets persecution, you will go through more persecution, and you will experience pandemonium. Your life will get crazy. But, if you go through it as a good soldier, God will give you joy! In this sermon, the deacons and the congregation were all told to just keep on serving because weeping may endure for a night, but joy/pleasure does come in the morning.

Survey Evaluation

Before hearing the sermons preached, some in the congregation believed that the deacon was supposed to be looked to as the one who provides the principal leadership of the church. They thought the deacon was the head of the pastor. Before receiving the information from the sermons, it was widely believed that the deacons held a position of leadership for the church. In reality, the deacons are to be a servant of the church. The tradition of the Black Baptist church is also the reason why the devotion service held the highest expectation for the deacon. The anticipated results of the survey, before the sermon series, were that the pastor should answer to the deacon. More anticipated results were that the congregation believed the deacon ran or oversaw the entirety of the church, and that no one had a higher position than the deacon.

The following charts encapsulate what the survey showed were the thoughts before the congregation was exposed to the preaching series. What the results were after the preaching/teaching is also shown on the following survey results. It should be noted, however, that these charts are the result of sermons delivered at the home church of the author of the project. This is to say that all the respondents were heavily predisposed to the preaching and teaching of the author, even before the time of the survey.

The Seven

TRADITION	TEACHING/PREACHING	RESULTS
The deacon must begin worship service with devotion, and he totally oversees the entire church.	The primary role of the deacon is to serve, not to oversee.	Most of the respondents said that the role of the deacon is to serve, not to oversee.
The deacon is the leader of the congregation. He tells people, including the pastor, what to do.	The deacon is to serve God by serving the people of God. He does this primarily by alleviating the pastor of certain duties.	The deacon is a servant of God by serving the people of God, and by helping the pastor.
Devotion service is a must, and it is the main responsibility of the deacon.	Visiting the sick is one responsibility of the deacon.	The responsibility of the deacon is to help the pastor serve the people of God.
The pastor is responsible to the deacon, specifically the Chairman of the Deacon Board.	The pastor is responsible to God, through the people of God. He is not responsible to the deacon, as such.	The pastor is responsible to God, not to the deacons.
The deacon is the head of the church; therefore, he isn't responsible to anyone.	The deacon is responsible to God, through the people of God, under the authority/leadership of the under-shepherd of the church, who is given by God.	The deacon is responsible to God and held accountable by the pastor.
The deacon runs/oversees the matters of the church.	The deacon does NOT run/oversee the church.	The deacon does NOT run/oversee the church.
The deacon oversees the pastor of the church.	The deacon does NOT oversee the pastor of the church.	The deacon does NOT oversee the pastor of the church.
With the changing of times, the office of deacon may not be as relevant and needed in the church of today.	Even with the changing of times, the office of deacon is still relevant and needed in the church of today.	With the changing of times, the office of deacon is still relevant and needed in the church.
The seven (7) of Acts 6 were deacons.	The seven (7) of Acts 6 were not "deacons," but they serve as the forerunner of this office.	The seven (7) of Acts 6 are examples of deacons today.

Chart 1

Chart 2: Primary Responsibility of the Deacon

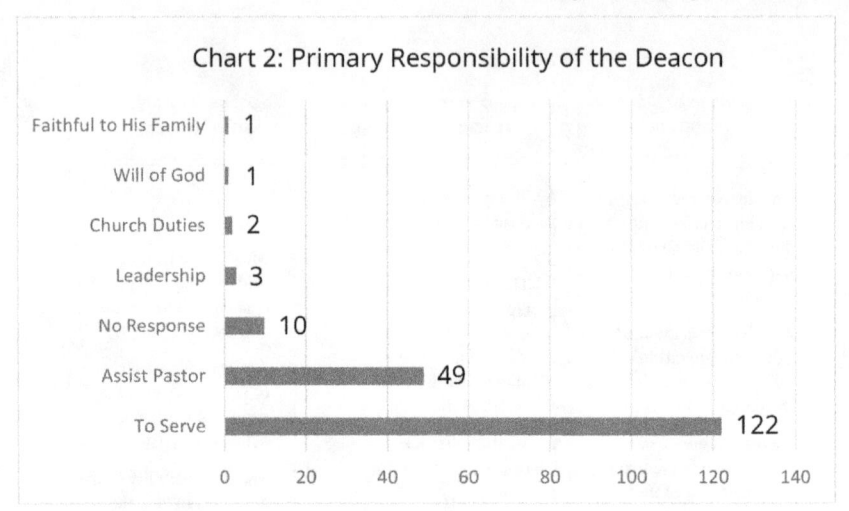

Category	Count
Faithful to His Family	1
Will of God	1
Church Duties	2
Leadership	3
No Response	10
Assist Pastor	49
To Serve	122

Chart 2 shows that 122 out of 188 responders to the question, "What is the primary responsibility of the deacon," answered that the responsibility of the deacon is to serve. Forty-nine responders to the question said that the deacon's responsibility is to assist the pastor, 10 responders chose "no response," while three said "leadership." Two responders replied, "church duties," with one responder each tallying a vote for the "will of God," and "faithful to his family."

Chart 3: Does the deacon oversee the pastor?

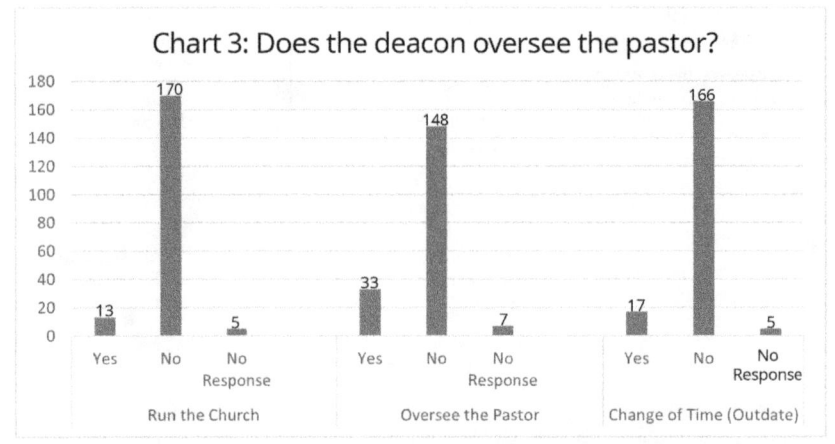

	Yes	No	No Response
Run the Church	13	170	5
Oversee the Pastor	33	148	7
Change of Time (Outdate)	17	166	5

Chart 3 shows that 170 responders out of 188 said that the deacon does not run/oversee the church. Thirteen said that the deacon does run the church, while five had no response. When

The Seven 65

asked if the deacon oversees the pastor, 148 said that the deacon does not oversee the pastor. Thirty-three responders said that the deacon does oversee the pastor, and seven replied with no response. When asked if the changing of time has made the office of deacon obsolete, 166 answered that the changing of time has not made the office of deacon obsolete. While 17 agreed that it has, five had no response.

Again, Chart 2, Chart 3, and Chart 4 are the results of the pre-sermon survey. They show the thoughts of the deacon/deacon ministry before the congregation was exposed to the preaching of the gospel on this subject. After hearing the four-sermon series, and the same survey was administered, Chart 5, Chart 6, and Chart 7 show the results after hearing the gospel about deacons.

Chart 4: Pastor-deacon relationship

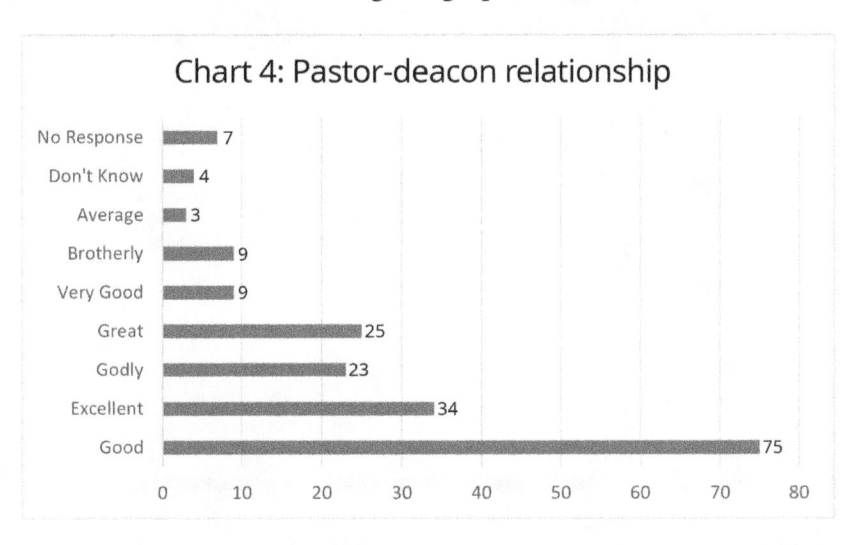

Category	Count
No Response	7
Don't Know	4
Average	3
Brotherly	9
Very Good	9
Great	25
Godly	23
Excellent	34
Good	75

Chart 4 details how the responders view the relationship between their pastor and deacon. Out of 188 responders, 75 answered that the relationship between their pastor and deacon was good. Thirty-four responders said that the relationship between their pastor and deacon was excellent, 23 classified it as Godly, and 25 said it was very good. Nine answered their pastor and deacon had a brotherly relationship, while nine more said the relationship was average. Four had a response of they did not know what kind of relationship existed between their pastor and deacon, and seven did not have a response at all.

Chart 5: Does the deacon oversee the pastor?

Change of Time (Outdate):
- No Response: 14
- Yes & No: 1
- No: 193
- Yes: 21

Oversee the Pastor:
- No Response: 8
- Yes & No: 2
- No: 138
- Yes: 81

Run the Church:
- No Response: 7
- Yes & No: 1
- No: 200
- Yes: 21

Chart 6: Primary Responsibility

- Faithful to His Family: 1
- Will of God: 1
- Church Duties: 2
- Visit Sick: 4
- Serve Congregation: 18
- Leadership: 18
- No Response: 27
- Assist Pastor: 110
- To Serve: 48

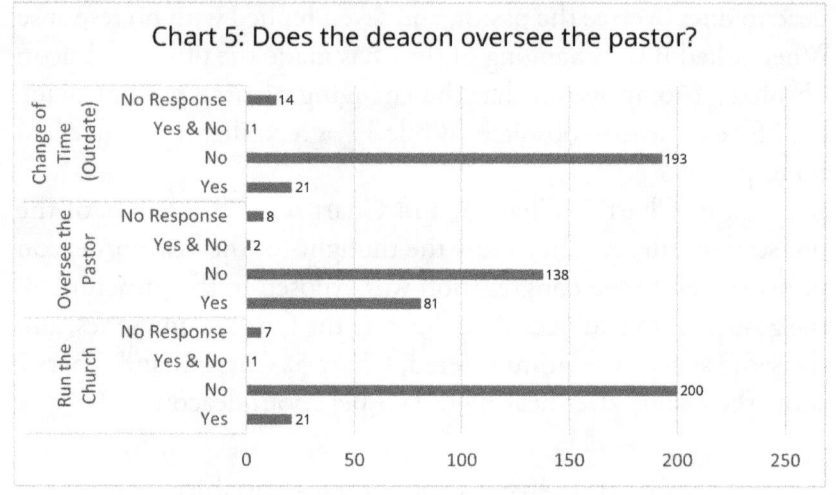

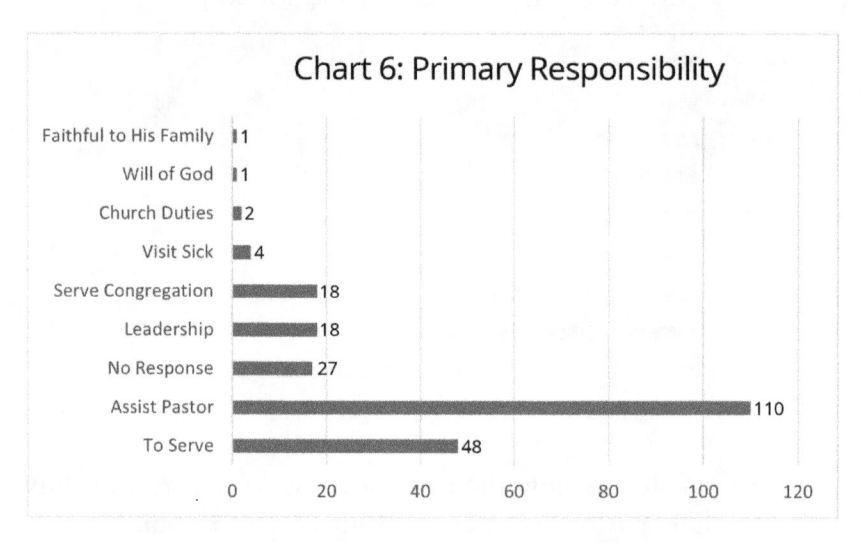

Chart 6 shows that 110 out of 229 responders to the question, "What is the primary responsibility of the deacon," answered that the responsibility of the deacon is to assist the pastor. Forty-eight responders to the question said that the deacon's responsibility is to serve, 27 responders chose "no response," while 18 said "leadership." Four people replied, "Visit the sick," with two responders saying,

The Seven

"Church duties," and one tallying a vote for each the "will of God," and "faithful to his family." An additional 18 votes were cast for, "serve congregation."

A total of 687 votes were cast for the questions regarding whether the deacon runs the church, oversees the pastor, and if the deacon ministry was outdated. Chart 6 shows that 200 responders out of 229 said that the deacon does not run/oversee the church. Twenty-one said that the deacon does run the church, one said, "Yes and no," while seven had no response. When asked if the deacon oversees the pastor, 138 said that the deacon does not oversee the pastor, eighty-one said that he does, two more answered, "yes and no," and eight had no response. When asked if the changing of time has made the office of deacon obsolete, 229 people responded, with 193 saying the changing of time has not made the office of deacon obsolete. While 21 agreed that it has, one said it has, but yet it hasn't, and 14 had no response.

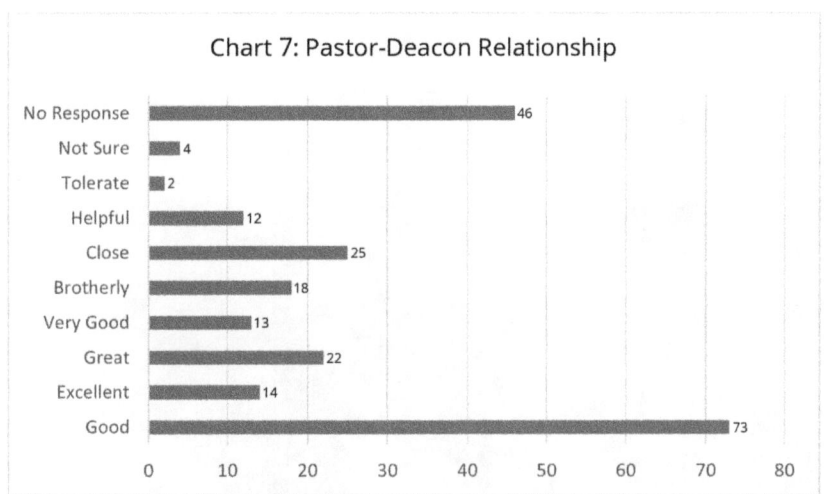

Chart 7: Pastor-Deacon Relationship

Category	Count
No Response	46
Not Sure	4
Tolerate	2
Helpful	12
Close	25
Brotherly	18
Very Good	13
Great	22
Excellent	14
Good	73

How do you describe the Pastor-Deacon relationship at your church?

Chart 7 again details how the responders view the relationship between their pastor and deacon. Out of 229 responders, 73 answered that the relationship between their pastor and deacon was good. Fourteen responders said that the relationship between their pastor and deacon was excellent, 22 classified it as great, and 13 said it was very good. Eighteen answered their pastor and deacon had a brotherly relationship, while 25 more said the relationship was close. Twelve people had responded that the relationship was "close," and two said it was "tolerate." Four votes were cast as being "not sure," and 46 people had no response.

CHAPTER FIVE
EVALUATING YOUR WORK: ARE YOU ON GOD'S PLAN?

After reading this book, it is possible for some to feel that the longevity of the consequences of slavery and the impending polity problems of the Black Church stand out to them. Then again, the implications of the longevity of the consequences of slavery may make some uncomfortable. Some may even express an exasperated relief when enlightened that the Black Church really had to be taught how to do "church." The Black Church was not the first church, so it makes sense that those who came before would teach those who followed the importance of positions, roles, and church expectations.

If nothing else, the work of this book has impressed upon me that several who may contemplate this subject matter for the first time may not have thought of or even spoken about this topic. Therefore, numerous readers of this work may be mentally liberated to hear how the deacon, who was not respected anywhere but the church, could exercise power that he ordinarily would not possess to wield. The very thought of the deacon not naturally acquiescing to the Bible-given authority of the pastor may speak volumes to the spiritual place (or lack thereof) that the deacon came from, and where he currently resides. This book has shown me that this reality is difficult to overcome – even 174 years after the founding of The

Historic John the Baptist. Hence, the strong residue of the lack of Biblical knowledge concerning the deacon within the universal Church altogether.

When confronted with the Word of God as it relates to this subject matter, every mind that is not changed is challenged to change. That is what the gospel does. The gospel challenges the hearer to see himself for what he is and to be compelled to change. When the challenge of the gospel is presented to deacons, their preconceived notions of power and their worldly-based ideas of leadership are whisked away to Henry Blackaby's crisis of belief.[86] At that point, the deacon is faced with the choice of either trusting God through His word, or not. The gospel brings him face-to-face with either leading the way society defines leadership (shouting directions and pointing fingers) or leading the way Jesus taught His disciples to lead, which was from behind and as a servant (Luke 22:24–27).

Nowhere was this on full display more than in the deacon classes that aided the fact-revelation mission for this book. In each class, the subtopic of humility is always stressed more than any other subtopic. In order to get every class started, the first thing asked of the students is to introduce themselves. Without fail, every man introduced himself with the title of "Deacon" before his given name. Moreover, this title was given with haughtiness, egotism, and superiority.

In chapter three we highlighted, perhaps, the most telling exchange I have had while teaching the subject matter of deacons. Suffice it to say, however, before each class is dismissed, the students are always asked to re-introduce themselves. In every circumstance, every man omitted his title when he gave his name. Using Luke 22:24–27 as a backdrop, we see that the Christian leader must exemplify humility and servanthood. This scripture is often the introduction to the class on becoming a Biblical deacon.

---

86 Henry Blackaby, Richard Blackaby, and Claude King, *Experiencing God: Knowing and Doing the Will of God* (Nashville, Tennessee: B&H Publishing Group, 2008), 207.

In the early church, the notions of humility and servanthood were the two cornerstones upon which the work centered. Without a formal education, or even the ability to read and write, the early deacons of the 19th century Black Church could have worked better with the traveling pastor if the deacon had more of a desire to possess humility and servanthood. For the 20th century deacon, the traditions passed down to him would have been worthless if he had also desired to possess more humility and a spirit of servanthood. Now within the confines of the 21st century, we again find ourselves with many deacons lacking humility. They are devoid of the desire to be servants. Whether it is the deacon of the part-time ministry or full-time ministry, the spirit of worldly leadership often still outweighs Biblical leadership. The tide is turning, however, and it is turning through Biblical training.

Workshop/Booklet Development

In each class, Acts 6:1–7 and 1 Timothy 3:8–13 are the two key Scriptures that are read and studied. The five-night class centers on a discussion stemming from these Scriptures. For clarification and ease of understanding, each night of the week is purposed for a specific part of the study. The following is a booklet compiled from reading/studying the aforementioned Scriptures, plus multiple other sources such as Webb's "Deacons: Servant Models in the Church," Naylor's "The Baptist Deacon," Hughes' "Acts: the Church Afire," McGee's commentaries on Acts and 1 Timothy, and various translations of the Bible, to name a few. These works have become favorites over a 25-year span of loving the ministry of deacons and desiring to see her flourish to the glory of God, and to the edification of the Body of Christ. The preferred style of teaching is an open, essay style of questioning that affords me, as the instructor, the freedom to exegete Scripture and to be flexible with student participation. In comparison to sermons in this setting, and the lecture style of teaching, both of which does not allow for midstream question-and-answering interaction, an open, essay style of questioning is inviting of back-and-forth interchange.

Conclusion

Although written for *Who Rules the Church*, I want to share this quote from Gerald Cowen:

> Deacons have a very important role in the church. Although they are servants, and their ministry is a ministry of service, the fact that they have been chosen demonstrates that the brethren respect them. Their role is second in importance only to the pastor. The Lord gives the pastor the responsibility of teaching the Word. Without this ministry, the church will not prosper spiritually. Part of the duty of the deacons is to relieve the pastor of responsibilities that would keep him from doing his best in studying the Word, spending time alone with God in prayer, and teaching the Word effectively. This is the reason the first deacons were chosen. Deacons still need to work closely with the pastor to make sure that this problem does not arise. Many churches are hampered in their spiritual development because the pastor has laid down the Word of God to do other things. The deacon is not described as a ruler in the church – rather as one who assists the overseers of the church and who the church appoints to fulfill specific ministries – but the deacon is, by virtue of his office, a leader of the church. His value to the church is in his service. He is not to be the pastor's supervisor, but his helper. Deacons are not to form a board to rule the church; that is not their job description. They are to lead the church in ministry. Churches who have such deacons will be blessed, indeed. Pastors who have such deacons to help them will be better pastors because of it. Deacons who serve well obtain for themselves a good standing and great boldness in the faith.[87]

Within this book, I have tried to take an age-old problem within the Black Baptist church and confront that problem with the gospel of Jesus Christ. The ministry of deacons needs to realize the power invested in it by and through the Word of God for the purpose of the church being successful. The success of the church

---

87 Gerald Cowen, *Who Rules the Church* (Nashville, Tennessee: Broadman and Holman, 2003).

is only attained with the Gospel of Jesus Christ permeating the entirety of the ministry of deacons. The deacon's ministry must get back to the Word of God.

While the deacon ministry of the church has operated in an unbiblical manner for almost 200 years, it is books such as this one that will challenge the worldly status and the traditional way of performing outside of the Bible's direction. And it can happen. The Deacons ministry of every congregation, regardless of the racial make-up of the congregation, will find its way back to the Biblical mandate that gave birth to her. The Word of God is the key.

In toiling through this project on the way to this book, I am convinced that the ministry of deacons continues to labor through toils because this ministry has relied on tradition more than God's Word. Deacon tradition says the deacon oversees the church. Deacon tradition says the deacon oversees the pastor. Tradition says the devotion period is more important than visiting the sick and shut-in. Tradition even says the deacon is the financial administrator of the church. All of this is unbiblical. The Bible does not uphold any of the things this tradition upholds.

With that said, I am in agreement with Cowen. Yes, the Biblical model for the deacon is to serve God by serving the man of God that God has placed as the under-shepherd of God's people. As the deacon serves God in this manner, making it easier for the pastor to lead God's people, the deacon would lead in ministry, and would obtain for himself a good standing and great boldness in the faith. However, it was found that many of the unbiblical traditions the Black Baptist deacon struggles with do find their genesis in the fact that the pastor was absent from the church. Therefore, in the absence of the pastor, the deacon "carried the water," as was noted from Traylor in chapter two. Indeed, the deacon ministry has allowed arrogance to replace humility, but the Word of God can restore misplaced humility, and thereby strengthen the people of God.

Teaching God's Plan to the Church

"The Results of Helping the Pastor"

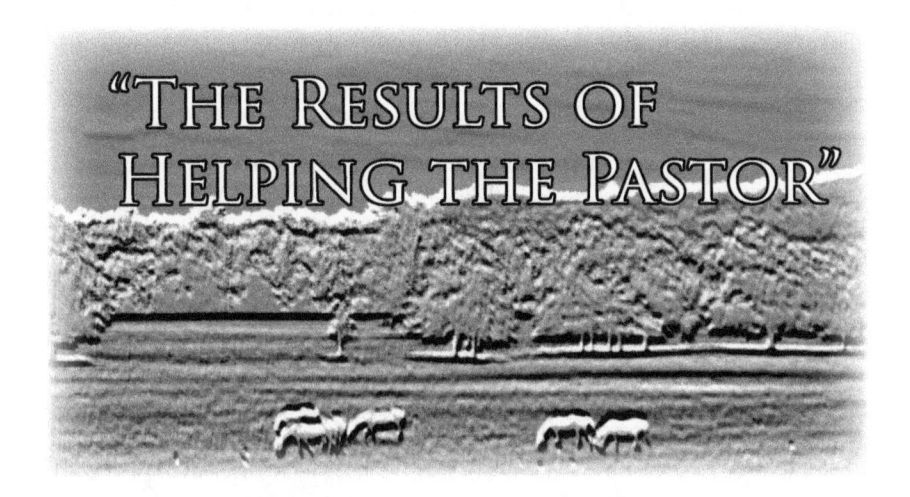

Acts 6:1–7

October 7, 2018
Greater Little Rock Baptist Church
Dissertation Survey for the Church/Deacon Ministry (Pre-survey #1)
8:00 a.m. & 10:45 a.m. Worship Services

One of the first books I read early into the pastoral ministry was *The Church Afire* by Dr. R. Kent Hughes. Written in 1996, Dr. Hughes takes on the book of Acts in a very, very detailed way and when he came to the opening subject of Acts chapter six, this is the way he opened his discourse (I want to share this with you; this is the way he started his conversation about the sixth chapter of Acts; listen):

Dr. Hughes said that when a certain Dallas church decided to split, each faction filed a lawsuit to claim the church property. The matter, unfortunately, made it to the courts, and a judge finally referred the matter to higher authorities in the particular denomination. A church court then assembled to hear both sides of the case and awarded the church property to one of the two factions. Of course, the losers then withdrew and formed another church in the area.

During the hearing, the church courts learned that the conflict had all begun at a church dinner when a certain elder received a smaller slice of ham than a child seated next to him. Sadly, this was reported in the newspapers for everyone to read. Just imagine how the people of Dallas laughed about that situation! This brought great discredit not only to that congregation, but to Jesus Christ! Listen. The tiniest events sometimes cause the greatest problems. Again, and again a church has warded off a frontal attack only to be undermined from within.

Acts 6 shows us Satan trying to disrupt the inward peace of the early church. Wonderful things were happening as the new church grew by leaps and bounds. Three thousand received Christ at Pentecost. Another 2,000 were added shortly thereafter. Acts 5 tells us that many more were then added to the church. Satan, unhappy about God's successes, sowed a spirit of murmuring and a seed of gossip among God's people, hoping to set believer against believer. Listen.

Countless works for God have been destroyed in this way. And as we move forward, Greater Little Rock, let us not forget that we are not above this same strategic attempt by this very same Satan.

As we move forward with the vision that God has blessed us with; as we consistently and faithfully plod down the road that will see us getting out of debt and that will see us burning our mortgage, let us not get too comfortable and forget that Satan will always try to knock us off track, just as he tried to knock the early church off track. Are you with me so far? Yes.

And we see exactly this in Acts 6. This is a perfect example of just how it really happens. This is everyday church life, right here in the first seven verses of Acts 6. You don't need Preachers of L.A. to show it to you. You don't need Preachers of Detroit to show it to you. You don't need Preachers of Atlanta, Preachers of Pensacola, or

The Seven 77

Preachers of Cantonment. You don't need any of those past, present and future television shows to show you what everyday ministry is all about because it is right here in front of your face right here in the Word of God. Here it is. This is the way ministry goes. Here it is. This is it! This is everyday church stuff, right here!

Whenever the church is doing something good to help somebody along the way; whenever the church is blessing people/children; whenever the church is blessing the elderly; whenever the church is feeding the hungry; whenever the church is clothing the naked; whenever the church is visiting the prisoners; whenever the church is warming the cold; whenever the church is cooling the hot; whenever the church is propping up the downtrodden; whenever the church is just trying to be a help to somebody else, the devil will always do his best to get insider the church, just so he can knock the church off the right track!

The devil doesn't mind us going to church as long as we stay in here, on the inside of the building, and do not go outside of the building in order to be a blessing to somebody else! The devil wants to knock us off track!

Yes, and that is what is going on in the background of the first seven verses of Acts 6. That is what's happening. Luke tells us in verse one that when the disciples were increasing in number there arose a complaint against the Hebrews by the Hellenists, because their widows were neglected in the daily distribution. And you know I want you to hold it right there. You have to hold up in order to marinate on the context of the scripture. Let's hold up right there.

Let's say it like this: in the days when the disciples were increasing in number, a complaint by the Hellenists came up against the Hebrews because the Hellenistic widows were being neglected in the daily distribution.

Well, let's go on a little further: (verses two-four) *and the twelve summoned the full number of the disciples and said, "it is not right that we should give up preaching the Word of God to serve tables. Therefore, brothers, pick out from among you seven men of good repute, full of the Spirit and of wisdom whom we will appoint to this duty/business. But we will devote ourselves to prayer and to the ministry of the Word."*

It always seems like just when things seem to be going well, something always happens. Doesn't it? Have any of you ever been there? The Apostle Paul said it like this…Paul said (*Romans 7:21*), "*I find it to be a law that when I want to do right, evil lies close at hand.*" The old folks used to say, "Every time I want to do good, evil is always present!

So, it really should not come as a surprise that when the number of disciples was multiplying, somebody in the church still found something to complain about! That is what happened, in today's vernacular. Yes. The church was going well. Things were well in the ministry. But all of a sudden, the pastors found out that things were not as well as they thought there were because somebody in the congregation felt mistreated.

And let me tell you something, those of you who may be new to church – listen. What we see here in Acts 6 is as real today as it was over 2,000 years ago. Help me somebody. I told you this is real stuff right here. Don't sleep on this.

Luke says that in the days when the disciples were increasing in number, a complaint arose. Listen. This word "complaint" is also translated as "quarrel," or "disagreement."

But as it is used by Luke in the text, this word could also refer to a secret murmuring that was not done openly. And there is where we mostly can identify with today's church.

I know you don't know this, but when I am asked in passing, "How is Greater Little Rock," my stand-pat answer usually is, "She is fine, as far as I know." And when I answer that way to someone who is in the church, they usually understand. But when someone who is not in the church should receive that answer from me, they are perplexed because they think the pastor knows everything that goes on in the church. You see, they don't know that sometimes there is a lot of secret murmuring that could go on in the church. Are you still with me? Yes.

The Seven

Secret murmuring was going on in the text because the Hellenists said that the Hebrews were not treating their widows right.

Now, just so you will know, Greek-speaking Jews is defined as Hellenists, while native Jews usually are defined as Hebrews. And so, what we really have is a conflict between folks who were considered "outsiders," and those who were considered, "originals." Do you hear me?

The Hellenists were the "outsiders," while the Hebrews were the "originals." The Hellenists were Jews, but they did not speak Aramaic. They spoke Greek. The Hebrews were "Jews." They lived in Jerusalem. They spoke Aramaic. So, don't miss this.

They both were Jews. They both were Jewish. The only difference was that one group did not live where the other group did. One group did not speak the way the other group spoke. One group did not act or live like the other group did so they were treated like second-class citizens, and their widows took the brunt of this action. Yes.

And now let's move to the 12, as Luke refers to them in verse two. Let's move to the 12 because the 12 figuratively stand in the shoes as pastor. And we say this because of the verses to follow. The 12 say, *"It is not right for us to give up preaching the Word of God to serve tables."* Hold up again. Don't miss this.

When the complaint came up, although it was murmured; although it was not said openly; although it was under the radar, murmuring always makes its way to the pastor because it is the pastor's responsibility to take care of the problem no matter when he finds out about it!

When the 12 hears about it, the first thing they did was to solicit some help. Listen. The pastor can't do it by himself. Listen.

I want to feed people who are hungry in this community, but I can't do it by myself. I want to clothe folks who need clothes, but I cannot do it by myself. I want to help children who are failing the first and the second and the third grade, but I cannot do it by myself. I want to help parents who are struggling to help their children, but I just can't do it by myself! The pastor needs somebody who is willing to help him in the ministry!

Some of you know that this passage is quite often used to enlighten on the ministry of deacons. And this sermon is not to say that using this passage is correct or incorrect to do so, but this sermon is only to point out what happens when someone steps forward (whether they are a deacon or not) to help the pastor in the ministry. That is what this sermon is for. And this sermon today is to point out what happens when someone steps forward and helps the pastor. That's what this is for.

And if you want to know what happens when folks step forward (deacons and non-deacons) to help the pastor then re-read verse seven – that's what happens. (Read it.)

You see, when news of the murmuring finally reached the 12, the first thing they noticed was their responsibility to fix it; to stop it. But they weighed the energy it would take in order to stop the murmuring with the energy it takes for them to be prepared in the ministry. Did you catch that? They counted it up. They weighed it out. Listen, again.

I said the 12 knew they were supposed to fix the problem; they knew they had to take care of the problem. There was a mess in the church and those who stood in the shoes as the pastor of the church knew that it was their responsibility to take care of the mess. And when they looked at it and they weighed the time it took to fix the mess, versus the time they needed to make sure they were good Bible-leaders, the 12 then said (verse two), "It is not desirable/right that we should leave the Word of God and work on this."

In other words, my Homeboy Study Edition Bible put it like this: "Ain't nobody got no time for that." And that is when they begin to look out in the congregation for somebody who was able to help them in the ministry!

And, again, I am not here to expound on the seven – that is for one of the upcoming sermons. I am not here to expound on Stephen, Philip, Prochorus, Nicanor, Timon, Parmenas or Nicolas. But I am here today simply to tell you that because they stepped up

The Seven

to help, the church grew! That is the first thing that happens when folks help the pastor **1) THE CHURCH GROWS**. Don't you see that? Well, that is the first thing that happens, and the second thing that happens is that **2) THE WORD GROWS**.

And, since I am already there, I'm going to go ahead and tell you that the third thing that happens is **3) THE LEADERS GROW**.

Those are the results of helping the pastor: the church grows, the Word grows, and the leaders grow.

Luke says the Word of God continued to increase (look at verse seven again), and the number of disciples multiplied greatly in Jerusalem! When someone helps the pastor, **THE CHURCH GROWS, THE WORD GROWS,** and **THE LEADERS GROW**! Listen.

The Apostles wanted to be able to spend more time praying than they did following foolish conversations! They wanted to spend more time in ministry than in mess! They wanted to spend more time with God than with childish folks!

When the pastor has help in the vision, in the plan of God, then the Word of God will continue to spread because the preaching of the Good News will be successful in winning the lost for Christ!

More and more will be saved because more will be able to hear. And when more can hear it is always because there is a man who will tell them what thus says the Lord! And this will always happen when somebody steps up to help the pastor lift up the name of Jesus!

I want you to see it. The church will grow. The Word will grow. And the leaders will also grow.

Please don't confuse the priest mentioned here in Acts 6:7 with those communal leaders of the Sanhedrin. These were priests, but they were not Sanhedrin priest. But, rather, they were priest who believed; they were leaders in the church, but they were not a part of the church of God. That is, not until they were able to hear an untiring Word of Truth out of the mouth of the Apostles.

And this is where I have to refer you to Paul again. I believe it is Romans 10:14 where Paul admonished: "How can they hear without a preacher?"

Church, when you step out of your comfort zone and trust the Lord to help the pastor in the ministry, you are even helping him to become stronger, and as he grows then those leaders who are blessed to hear will also grow, and those who need to be converted will be converted!

I believe the Lord when He said (at Isaiah 55:11), "So shall My word be that goes forth from My mouth; it shall not return to Me void, but it shall accomplish what I please, and it shall prosper in the thing for which I sent it."

Church, if we work in the ministry together…if we pray together; if we give together; if we have faith together; if we worship Him together; if we lift Him up together; if we are patient together; if we are committed together, then the church would grow, and the Word of God would grow, and even leaders would grow…because this is what happens when you help the man of God in ministry! Now, here is the last question before we go.

Is there anybody here who can love the Lord enough to help in the ministry?

And before you answer, here is what I know: I know I reap what I sow. And so I know, that if I help you, one day somebody is going to help me!

So, let me just say it like Mahalia said it: If I can help somebody, as I pass along; if I can cheer somebody, with a word or son; if I can show somebody that he is traveling wrong, then my living shall not be in vain.

I'm through, but my living shall not be in vain.

When you help the pastor, **THE CHURCH GROWS, THE WORD GROWS,** and **THE LEADERS GROW!**

"What the Deacon - and Everybody - Should Know"

Acts 6:8–15; 7:54–60

October 14, 2018
Greater Little Rock Baptist Church
Dissertation Survey for the Church/Deacon Ministry (Pre-survey #2)
8:00 a.m. & 10:45 a.m. Worship Services

As we continue on this trek of preaching and teaching on our subject matter, I cannot do so without moving into Acts 7 a little because the new subject that begins at verse eight (8) of Acts 6 shifts into something a little more dramatic.

(And) I say dramatic because surely one cannot read and understand what exactly is going on here without sensing the drama in all of this. I mean, when you read Acts 6 and you come down to verse eight (8), surely you cannot stop reading until you would have read all of chapter 7. I mean, the drama is just too much. Yeah. Why am I so dogged and so persistent in this?

Well, I am doggedly persistent in this because every Christian ought to know what happens when you try to live like Jesus. Listen to me now. I said every last one of you who knows that you are a Christian, should know and be aware of the fact that when you try to live like Jesus; when you endeavor to be an example of Christ; when you try to be a good Christian; when you make up in your mind that you are going to try to live right; when you finally come to yourself and you determine that you are going to try to talk right and you want to try to walk right and you want to try to live right; when you make up your mind to stop those habits that you know are killing you; when you make up your mind to stop smoking and you are going to stop drinking; when you make up your mind to delete some friends; when you know that you need to un-friend some folks on Facebook.

When you make up your mind that you are going to stand for Jesus, no matter who does not stand and no matter who does stand; when you make up your mind that YOU are going to stand up for the Lord, there are some things that you must be sure that you know that you know! Am I right?

Well, can I tell you the way Ruth Caye Jones said it? Sister Jones said it like this. You know, it was during some awful days of WWII and Sister Jones was a housewife who suddenly had to stop her housework because the Holy Spirit was speaking to her. She felt the presence of the Lord and from His presence she began to put pen to paper and Ruth Caye Jones said: "In times like these, you need a Savior, in times like these, you need an anchor; so be sure, be very sure, your anchor holds and grips the Solid Rock!"

Does anybody know what she was talking about? Does anyone know who she was talking about? Well, just in case, Ruth Caye Jones said, "The Rock is Jesus, yes, He is the One, this Rock is Jesus, the only One. Be very sure. Be very sure, your anchor holds and grips the solid Rock!"

Church, when your world starts to rocking and reeling; when your friends turn their backs on you; when it seems like you are not going to make it; when you have more bills than money; when your world seems like it is upside down; when you just cannot seem to get up on your feet (who am I talking to in here?); when it seems like it is just one thing after another, after another; when family lets you down; when friends let you down; when your church lets you down; when you let yourself down; there are some things that you better be sure that you know that you know that you know! Have any of you ever been there?

Have you ever been to that place where you felt all alone? Have you ever been to that place where you felt no one cared; no one understood? Have you been to that place where you felt nobody got it? Have you been to that place and felt like you were there all by yourself?

Well, whenever you get to that place you better be sure that you know that you know who your anchor is connected to! Listen.

If you don't know that you know what you know, then you will never be able to stand up for Jesus. And being a Christian is all about standing up for Jesus. But if you are going to stand for Him, then you are going to have to know some stuff. Are you with me today?

I told you that verse eight turns our subject matter around and that it also turns us into a more dramatic scene. Look at it with me if you don't mind.

In the first seven verses we are told that the congregation had a problem and the problem was brought to the pastors of the church (we can call them that). The apostles were told the problem, but they quickly surmised that for them to take care of the problem meant that they would have to stop spending time preaching the Word of God. Look at verse two. It's right there. And now look at verse four. If they had to deal with this, it would have taken away from their prayer time and from the ministry of the Word. They said it's not right.

But because the problem still needed to be answered, what the apostles did was to commission the crowd to look out and find seven men of good reputation, full of the Holy Spirit, and full of wisdom whom could be appointed over this kind of business. And the first man that Luke named as being a part of this crowd is a man by the name of Stephen.

For those of you who may still think the Bible is *just* a book, I submit to you that it is not by coincidence that Stephen is listed first out of the seven in verse five. Oh, no, no, no. Those of you who have sat under my teachings for any number of these almost 14 years should know at least two things about my personal ministry by now. Number one, we don't call my wife "First Lady." That's not fair to her, and it's not fair to you. That is a secular term that doesn't belong around the neck of the Body of Christ. That's number one.

And number two about me, is that I do not believe in luck or coincidences. No, I don't. I cannot believe in coincidences because I believe God has a plan, and I believe He put His plan into motion the day He declared, "Let there be light." God is the only will in the universe that matters, and His will is either perfect or permissive!

In other words, God will either make certain things happen, or He will allow certain things to happen. But, either way, no matter what happens to me, it is never by coincidence, but it is all in God's plan for my life! I trust Him!

And I see His plan with Stephen being listed first because at verse eight Luke begins to go into detail about this Stephen, and the first thing Luke says about him is that Stephen was full of faith and power, and he was doing great wonders and signs among the people.

Can I bless the person sitting closest to you? Let me bless the person closest to you. Listen.

Stephen quickly found himself in the middle of a lot of trouble. He was picked out to be picked on. He was in big trouble and he seemingly did not have any help. Some former slaves rose (verse nine) and disputed with Stephen. And then they trumped up false witnesses (verse 11) against him. And then they stirred up the people against him and they seized him, and they brought false witnesses and they brought him before the council, and they lied on him. But then, when they gazed at him while on the witness stand (verse 15), all who sat in the council saw that his face was like the face of an angel. Now let me tell you why I think that was the case:

Verse eight says that Stephen was full of faith and he was full of power.

Verse 10 says he was full of wisdom.

Church, when you have that kind of faith in God, and you have the power of God, and you have the wisdom of God, I believe you will also have the presence of God! Listen.

God will never leave His children alone! When you are all by yourself, you really are not by yourself, for if you are a child of God, they can lie on you all they want to – let them lie!

Have any of you ever been lied on? They can talk about you all they want to talk – let them talk! Have you ever been talked about? They can criticize; they can scandalize; they can idealize; they can glamorize; they can romanticize — whatever they want to do. But they cannot deny that you have the presence of your God because God will never leave His children alone!

Here it is, children. Here it is:

We have read the end of the story. We know that this angry mob stones Stephen to death. You have read this. We have just read this together. So, you already know that Stephen knows how you have felt. You know now that Stephen could identify with you. When you have felt all alone, Stephen knows how you felt. When you felt like no one cared. Stephen knows how you felt. He was stoned. He was stoned until he died. You know that, so that is not what this is about. Ultimately, this lesson is about what he knew that helped him to make it through those trials. This is about what Stephen knew that gave him strength to make it through that circumstance. And what Stephen knew is the same thing they you and I need to know in order to make it through the rough times that we will go through as well. Listen. The first thing I want to show you is that if we are going to make it through as Stephen did, we must **KNOW THE WORD OF GOD**.

The clue to this — the key to this is in Acts 7:54. Look at it. It says, "Now when they heard these things they were enraged, and they ground their teeth at him." (NKJ – "gnashed at him with their teeth.") Stop right there. Don't go too far. Don't miss this:

There is only one thing that can make them this upset with Stephen. Do you know what that is? I promise you. There is only one thing – in the world – that can make them so upset that they would want to tear him to pieces with their teeth: one thing — the Word of God. Listen.

Folks are fine with you on your job until you start talking that God stuff. Folks are fine with you in your family until you start talking that Bible stuff. Folks will even like you, they will be friendly towards you, they will play with you and will befriend you if you keep your God in your pocket.

But I want you to know right now today, that as soon as you start saying what the Lord has done for you — as soon as you start witnessing about how the Lord has brought you out…as soon as you start witnessing and raising your hand because the Lord has been good to you, those very same folks that you thought were your friends will turn their backs on you, and they will drop you like a bad habit!

Where am I getting this from? Well, Luke says, "When they heard 'these things.'" What things, Wesley? What things? Well, it's the Word of God!

The Word of God says, "these things," for if you go back to Acts 7:2, there you will find Stephen spreading the Word of God. Yeah. That's what he was doing. He was spreading the Word of God!

And, no, I am not one of those preachers who say that Deacons are preachers, but what I am is one of those Christians who believe that ALL Christians should know the Word of God! And you don't have to be a preacher to know the Word! You don't have to be a preacher to proclaim the Word! You don't have to be a preacher to spread the Word! Listen. All of God's children should know the Word! Stephen knew the Word. He told them about Abraham and about Joseph and about Moses. He told them about Joshua and about David.

But he also told them that they were full of sin and were a stiff-necked people. Stephen knew the Word, and church, we should also know the Word!

We should know that in the beginning, God created the heavens and the earth! We should know that God made man, and then God

The Seven 89

made woman! We should know that God intended for man and woman to be together! We should know that mankind sinned! We should know that God punished mankind! We should know that the sin of mankind took us away from God! But we should also know that because God loves us so much.

We should know that because God loves us so much, that He decided to give us a way back to Him! And that way back is named, Jesus! We should know that Jesus is the Way! We should know that by no other name can man be saved — but at the name of Jesus!

Every Christian ought to know something about Jesus!

Stephen shows us that we ought to **KNOW THE WORD**, but we should also **#2) KNOW WHERE TO LOOK**.

If we tell the truth, church, when we get into trouble, most of the time we will start looking into the wrong places. Come on. Tell the truth. And when we look in the wrong places, we will invariably see the wrong things. Come on, now. Tell the truth.

But Luke says in verses 55–56, that when Stephen was in trouble, he knew where to look. Where did he look? When Stephen was in trouble, he gazed up into heaven, and he saw the glory of God and Jesus standing at the right hand of God. And then Stephen said, "Behold, I see the heavens opened, and the Son of Man standing at the right hand of God."

Now, this may not mean anything to you, but I know that scripture usually only shows Christ *sitting* at the right hand of God. Scripture usually only says that Jesus is or will be *sitting* at the right hand of His Father. But right here, for Stephen, Stephen said that he saw Jesus STANDING at God's right hand! I thought you would get that. Maybe I was wrong. Okay.

When Jesus saw His servant, suffering for His sake; when Jesus saw His child, being beaten, for no fault of his own; when Jesus saw His boy going through these trials, although he did nobody wrong, I see where Jesus was not able to keep His seat, but Jesus stood to His feet as if to welcome His child on home!

Church, if you want to see Jesus when you are going through tough times in your life, you have to know where to look! He is not going to be in the beer bottle! He is not going to be in the crack house! You will not find Him in the middle of confusion! But if you want to see Him, you have to look to the hills – from whence comes your help? Well, all of your help; I said all of your help — when you are in trouble, you need some help, and all of your help — you have to look to the One who is the author and the finisher of your faith! I said all of your help — just know where to look.

And then, lastly, you have to **KNOW THE WORD**, and you have to **KNOW WHERE TO LOOK**, then you have to **#3) KNOW WHAT TO SAY**.

(Verses 59–60) As they were stoning Stephen, Stephen cried out, "*Lord Jesus, receive my spirit.*" And falling to his knees he cried out with a loud voice, "*Lord, do not hold this sin against them.*" And when he had said this, he fell asleep.

The chosen men of Acts 6 were not called "Deacons," per se, but we certainly can look to them as being the forerunner of those who held the office of deacons. And, a more important part of that is the fact that this man was (as all deacons and Christians should be) just like Christ. Yes. This Christian was just like Christ. Stephen lived his last days just like the One in whom he trusted. He lived his last minutes like the One in whom he believed.

Stephen knew whom his enemies were, but he did not wish them ill, but he prayed that they would be forgiven, just like His Savior prayed.

While they were stoning him, he prayed. He knew what to say. He knew that he had been blessed with a great amount of faith, and he knew that his enemies needed grace. So, Stephen prayed. He knew what to say.

He knew that since God had given him another chance, then he was expected to pray for his enemies to also get another chance. Do I have a witness?

If you know that the Lord has been good to you, how can you not wish for Him to be good to someone else? You have to know what to say.

If God has given you grace — if God has given you another chance — if God has looked over your faults and has supplied your needs — if God has been good to your children — if God has given your grandchildren another chance — if God has been waking you and your family up every morning.

What kind of people do you think we are? We don't repay evil for evil. We don't live like the heathen live. We don't do what the unbeliever does, but we strive to live like Christ, and I heard Christ say, when He was being mistreated — when He was being lied on — when He was being talked about — when He was being persecuted — when He was being cussed out — when He was being beat up — He said, "Father, forgive them, for they don't know what they are doing."

We don't talk the way other folks talk! We want to bless because we want God to bless us! Whenever we are up against a trouble, we need to know the Word, we need to know where to look, and we need to know exactly what to say!

"Thank God for the Deacon"

1 Timothy 3:8–13

October 21, 2018
Greater Little Rock Baptist Church
Dissertation Survey for the Church/Deacon Ministry (Pre-survey #3)
8:00 a.m. & 10:45 a.m. Worship Services

Of all of the things and of all of the situations and of all of the people who have traditionally been picked at and picked on in the church, from where I stand in my part of the world, the deacon runs a close second – right behind the preacher.

And you don't have to have an extensive church background to come close to agreeing with me. All you have to do is visit a barber shop or a hair salon. Go to a family reunion or, better yet, just join the church – any congregation – the deacon is right behind the pastor when it comes to gossip and jokes. And, depending on the deacon and depending on the pastor, sometimes the deacon may be first in line sometimes (with the pastor second) when it comes to who is talked about the most.

Yes, traditionally, the devil has done a very thorough job; he has done a particularly good job in convincing even those of us who are in the church that all deacons and all pastors are nothing but punch lines. And because of this, the devil has been able to steal joy from the church because the church has forgotten just how much the Lord loves the deacon! And check this out: the deacon is important to the Lord and to the church. God loves the deacon.

I wish every Baptist knew that there are only two (2) Biblical offices in the church: the pastor and the deacon. That's it. It's only two (2). We have trustees because Caesar said we need Trustees. We have ushers to help us to be more organized in our seating. We have security and we have parking attendants because we want to be as safe as we can be. We have greeters because we want to be as nice as we can be. But we have pastors and deacons because the Lord told us that is whom He wants us to have. That is whom the church needs to have. That is whom we are supposed to have!

But today is not about the pastor. Today is about the deacon. And for those of you who do not know, the word from which we get our word "deacon," is a word that literally means "servant." "Deacon" means "servant." It comes from the Greek work *diakonos*, which is a standard ancient Greek word meaning "servant," or "minister," or "messenger." Listen. He runs errands. He cares for the poor. He is a waiter/server like one who waits on and serves a dinner table. He is a teacher/minister/servant. The deacon has no administrative duties. He has no oversight expectations. The deacon is a servant.

You know I am doing my work and as a part of my project I have to interview some folks, and one of my interviews was with Dr. Jerry Young (Dr. Young is the President of the National Baptist Convention) and he reminded me that the word for deacon, *diakonos*, breaks down to show that "*dia*," meaning "through," and "*konos*," means "the dust." So, *diakonos* shows us the deacon is one who literally runs to serve – so fast – that he kicks up dust on his way to serving.

The deacon wants to serve somebody so badly; he wants to help somebody so much that you can see dust from his heels as he runs just to have the opportunity to serve!

And I think that is where all the lines get crossed up. I think that is the onus of the communication problem between church and deacon, or between people and deacon, between community and deacon. You see, traditionally, because the pew has not correctly understood what it means to be a deacon; the deacon has thusly been expected by the people to do some things that God has never expected him to do!

Look at it. Traditionally, most of us know, the people have expected the deacon to be the leader, when that is not what the Lord has expected him to be. The Lord has expected him to be a servant!

And I am not here to get into the socio-economic reasons and the racial reasons and the traditional reasons why he has been wrongly expected to be something that he was never intended to be. This is not the sermon for that. But I am here to set the record straight that most congregations have not been fair to the office of deacon because they have asked the deacon to lead when the Lord has instructed him to follow!

And you know I am dying to show it to you, don't you? I'm dying to show it to you. I cannot wait to show it to you. But before I do, I have to say this one more time: I love deacons. I do. I love the ministry of Deacons. I pray that when the Lord allows me to retire as your pastor that I will be able to serve Him as a deacon on my way to Heaven. Yes, I do. I don't know who my pastor is going to be at that time, but I want to bless my pastor. I do. You see, I have messed around and I have learned a few things and one of the things I have learned is that when you bless the man of God; when you bless the people of God; when you work in ministry and you are a blessing to the children of God, the Lord will never allow you to do more for Him, then what He will do for you. I wish somebody would learn that. Listen.

If you want to be blessed, all you have to do is to lose yourself in an attempt to be a blessing to somebody else. That's all you have to do.

If you give, the Lord will not rest until He gives back to you more of what you have given to others. And I am moving on, but I have to say this: this is why I am so sure that we are going to continually be blessed, because I have so much seed in the ground around Greater Little Rock — I'm telling you. You have no idea. I have planted seeds and I know that the God I serve will never allow His child to plant in faith and not yield in the future. I know that, and so I easily equate that with the office of deacon because serving is another way of just planting seeds! Do you see that? Well, let me try to show this to you through the way the Apostle Paul put it.

Paul, in his letter to young Timothy, told the young preacher/pastor in 1 Timothy 3, that he (Timothy) should find men of the congregation that meet certain requirements to be a deacon (look at verse eight). Paul says that the deacon must be reverent. He must not be double-tongued. He cannot be given to much wine. The deacon cannot be greedy for money. And he must (in verse nine) hold the mystery of the faith with a pure conscience. But let us stop right here and take a breather before we finish this up. Check this out.

It does not take a seminary degree to see that what is mentioned in verse eight are all negative in connotation. If you look at closely, I know you will see it and will agree with me. This is universal. There are four qualifications there in verse eight and all four of them are negative in their connotation. Paul says the deacon should be reverent (1), not double-tongued (2), not given to much wine (3) and not greedy for money (4). That is four qualifications right there, and all four of them are negative in their connotations. I hope you see. OK.

But then in verse nine, a positive connotation is embedded because Paul says that the deacon should be able to hold the mystery of the faith with a pure conscience. And then if we just skip verses 10–11 just for a second, I want to show you something by adding verse 12 in this first. Look at this. By looking at verse eight and

The Seven

seeing a negative connotation, and then looking at verses nine and 12 together, I now see a positive connotation that says to me that it is the character of the deacon that God desires to use more than the capabilities of the deacon! I hope you see it. **Character means more than capability.**

Even if it is not there, I hope you have eyes to see it because nowhere does the Word of God mention any kind of special capabilities the man needs to have in order to be a deacon. He does not have to be an educator. He does not have to hold degrees. He does not have to be a specialist in any particular area of life/society.

No matter how many degrees he has; it doesn't matter how much money he makes; it does not matter how well he can speak or what he may drive. All that really matters is that he is always able to be a servant!

And let me tell you something — an undignified man cannot be a servant. To be reverent is to be dignified. You must be worthy of respect. You must be of a serious mind about spiritual issues.

In other words, you can't be silly all the time, but you must know how to carry yourself. Clean yourself up. Put your Sunday-go-to-meeting clothes on and know how to talk to folks sometimes — if you want to be a good servant. Be reverent! Act like you've got some sense, sometimes!

And then he said to not be double-tongued. In other words, you can't say one thing to one somebody over here and then turn around and say something else to one somebody over there and think you are a good deacon. That does not work like that. That's being double-tongued. But you must be sincere. Your word must be reliable. Your "yes" must be "yes," and your "no" must be "no." Your word must be your bond. The deacon cannot be double-tongued.

And this third one may be my favorite one because this is one of the more misunderstood ones: given to much wine. And in order to understand this you have to know how to correctly read it. If you read it wrongly, you will understand it wrongly. And I know there are a lot of theologians who do not agree with my interpretation of this, but this is my interpretation. I know we differ. Some of you may even differ but this is the way I understand it. Listen.

Paul does not say the deacon cannot be given **too much** wine. But he says the deacon cannot be given **to** much wine. In other words, the deacon can drink a little wine, but **he cannot be GIVEN to wine**. Notice the word usage. This is not too; this is not two; this is to.

Too means also; in addition to; exceedingly. Two means one more than one; double. To means a destination; near; towards.

So, in other words, wine cannot control him. He cannot be given to it. It cannot overtake him. Do you see the difference? Yes.

And then Paul admonished that the deacon must not be greedy for money. In other words, he should not do anything in the ministry for the sake of money. Yes.

But church, you know if we are going to have a chance at being as blessed by all of this as we would like, we have to dig a little deeper than what we see right here. Am I right? Yes. And in digging just a little deeper, I believe we can find what was driving Paul's ability to write these words. Yes, I do. And we don't have to dig far. We only have to go back less than a month – back to the sermons I've been preaching – because it was in Acts 7:58 where we saw where Stephen was being stoned to death, those who stoned him until he died did so after they laid their cloaks at the feet of a young man named Saul.

Church, I believe that is why Paul is the absolute best person to be able to tell Timothy about what a deacon should look like because it was Paul, who was then named Saul, who aided in the murder of one of the precursors/forerunners to the office of deacon.

Even if Stephen were not a deacon, I believe he and Philip, and Prochorus, and Nicanor, and Timon, and Parmenas, and Nicolaus all were forerunners of what would be called deacons. And so, since Paul saw what this office really looked like; since he experienced what good deacons should do; since he had knowledge of what deacons should say and where deacons should look; since Paul saw the lifestyle; he saw Stephen live like Christ. He heard Stephen talk like

The Seven

Christ. He witnessed Stephen die like Christ. So now, I believe that Paul is qualified to describe how every deacon should strive to be!

And he includes the whole of the family life of the deacon. He includes his whole life. He says (in verse 10) the deacon should be tested and given the opportunity to prove himself.

And then Paul says that the wife of the deacon must also help him out. And right there, let me say this: It is impossible to be a good deacon and not have a good wife. The wife of the deacon, much like the wife of the pastor, can either make you or she can break you. Paul said the wife of the deacon must be dignified, not a slanderer. She must be sober-minded and faithful in all things. Listen.

The wife of the deacon must be strong! And I include in that, she must let her husband be the man of the house! Paul said the deacon must manage his children and his own house well! For those who serve well as deacons gain a good standing for themselves and also great confidence in the faith that is in Christ Jesus.

Now, you can't tell me that Paul was not thinking of what he saw when he was a younger man when he wrote that. I just believe he did. I believe Paul began to recall how when Stephen fell to the ground (Acts 7:60), he heard Stephen cry out with a loud voice, *"Lord, do not hold this sin against them."*

I believe that is why Paul said that the deacon who serves well gains for himself a good standing and a great boldness in the faith that is in Christ Jesus.

Pastor Mark Dever, the longtime pastor of Capitol Hill Baptist Church in Washington, D.C., (also the founder of 9 Marks Ministries), in one of his blogs Dr. Dever says the deacon is both a shock-absorber and a servant.

He is a shock-absorber because (according to the teachings of Acts 6), the forerunners to the office of deacons literally stepped in and took the shock; they absorbed it; they did the work in the middle of the congregation, keeping it off the pastor, which allowed the pastor to keep his mind on the preaching of the Word. He is a shock-absorber.

And he is a servant. He serves. That's what he does. He serves.

The deacon doesn't look to be served — but he serves.

And that is why I thank God for the office of deacon. That is why I thank God for the deacon, because **SERVANTS EQUAL PROGRESS**. Do I have a witness?

When I was a boy, I used to hear the old folks say, whenever the job seemed to be bogged down — someone would say, "It seems like we have too many chiefs, and not enough Indians." They would say, "Everybody wants to be the chief; nobody wants to be the Indian."

I didn't know what they were talking about at that time. I have always loved cowboys and Indians. To me, the Indian lost too many times. To me, I wanted the Indian to win, sometimes. But as I got older, I begin to learn that the old folks were not disparaging the so-called Indian. They were saying that everybody wanted to be in charge, but nobody wanted to work! Everybody has something to say about it, but nobody wants to do anything about it!

So, I thank God for the servant, because he who serves well — he who doesn't have to be out front — he who doesn't have to hear his name called — he who doesn't have to be right all the time — he who doesn't have to get his way — he who doesn't to give the orders — that is the same one who will hear his God say, "Well done, my good and faithful servant!"

Can I tell you one more thing? You don't have to be a deacon to hear that! All you have to do is just be a servant! Just be willing to be in the background!

Just be willing to be talked about. Just be willing to be lied on. Just be willing to work when nobody else is working. Just be willing to bless the Lord by serving His people. Just be willing to follow leadership.

Just be willing to serve Him and you will hear, "Well done!"

"When Serving Meets Persecution"

Acts 8:1–8

December 2, 2018
Greater Little Rock Baptist Church
Dissertation Survey for the Church/Deacon Ministry (Pre-survey #4)
8:00 a.m. & 10:45 a.m. Worship Services

 In his timeless and rich masterpiece, The Cost of Discipleship, that great German theologian, Dietrich Bonhoeffer said, "When Christ calls a man, he bids him come and die." And that, my friends, sums up Acts 7, and it bridges all the way to Acts 8 for us today.
 In light of the fact that we have not been able to connect these dots without interruption, let me just once again repeat Bonhoeffer's words as we turn our attention to what happens when serving meets persecution. Bonhoeffer said, "When Christ calls a man, he bids him come and die."

Just in case you are just joining us, or if your memory is challenging, let me tell some and remind others that we are in the middle of looking at what the deacon is. We are learning about deacons.

The last time I was blessed to talk to you out of this book saw us leave with the visual of Stephen being stoned to death by those who did not want to hear him lift Jesus. And there is exactly where I must start with you today. I must start around the fact that Stephen was stoned to death all because he lifted the Savior of the church. Do you hear me this morning? I said Stephen was stoned to death. He was killed. He was punished. Stephen was persecuted. He was persecuted. Why? Because Stephen was a lifter of the Savior! Stephen was a servant.

If you are a Christian — if you have been born-again — if you know that you know that were you to stop breathing in your sleep tonight you would go to heaven because you have already confessed your sins and you have already believed in your heart that God raised Jesus from the grave, and you know that you know that you are saved, then you might as well know and become even more familiar with the fact that whenever you lift up Jesus, you will be persecuted.

Does anybody know that today? Listen.

The devil will not stop until he gets somebody to lie on you if you lift up Jesus. He will not rest until he messes with your job if you lift up Jesus. He will not slow down until he starts some mess in your family if you lift Jesus. The devil will have to do everything within his power just to try to get you to turn around and go back to where you came from if you dare to lift Jesus. What does that mean? Well, church, you will be persecuted if you are not ashamed to worship the Lord your God!

You will be persecuted. You will be wronged. You will be mistreated. You will be victimized. You will be offended. You will be injured. Your feelings will be hurt. You will be insulted. You will get upset. You will be snubbed. When you dare to give God glory — when you dare to give Him the praise— when you have the courage to stand up for Jesus — when you have the nerve/guts to worship Him, in spite of your circumstances — in spite of the way you feel — if you still have the mindset to say, "Thank you, Jesus," even when you are being talked about; "glory, hallelujah," even when you don't know what your job is going to do; whenever you step out on faith and give God glory – in advance – before anything looks like it's going to happen, I want you to know right now, you will be persecuted!

Just ask Stephen. But, wait. You cannot ask Stephen because Stephen was persecuted. He lifted the Savior. Stephen was a servant. And because Stephen was a servant of the Savior of the church, Stephen was persecuted.

That is the end of chapter 7, and it takes us to where we start today at chapter 8. As Stephen kneeled and prayed for his attackers, Luke says that Saul was consenting (Acts 8:1) to his death.

Before I move on, let me say it one more time – if you are going to be a servant of the Savior, Stephen shows us that you will be persecuted. Am I right about this? Yeah.

Being a Christian is not easy. You will be persecuted. This is not for the faint of heart. You will be talked about. You will be lied on. You will be misunderstood. Things are going to happen to you in this life. You will be persecuted. Am I right about it?

Well, if you are unsure, I am prepared to strengthen my case. I came prepared to tell some and remind others that this same Saul, after he was renamed Paul, would eventually learn and he shared with Timothy (2 Timothy 2:12), that *if we suffer, we shall also reign with him; if we deny him, he also will deny us.*

But even more so than that, Jesus told us it would happen. He told us. And Jesus even sweetened the pot for us when (not if) it happen. He said it would happen. He said it had to happen. And so I am glad that Jesus declared at Matthew 5:10–12 (it's in the Beatitudes where He shows us). Jesus declared: "*blessed are they who are persecuted for the sake of righteousness, for theirs is the kingdom of heaven; blessed are you when they insult you and persecute you and utter every kind of evil against you falsely because of me. Rejoice and be glad, for your reward will be great in heaven; for thus they persecuted the prophets who were before you."*

Church hold your head up when things don't go your way. Stick your chest out when you are called everything but a child of God. Wave your hand in adoration when haters are on your track. Jesus said despite all these things, you will still be blessed! You will still be able to smile! You will still be able to hold your head up! You will still be able to see the bright side! And then, when it's all over down here, He said that great will be your reward in heaven! So, go ahead — tell your persecutors to go ahead and give it their best shot, because what the devil meant for bad, tell them you serve a God who can turn it around for your good!

Stephen was persecuted because he was a servant of the Savior of the church. And now let me tell you what happens to us when we are this kind of servants. What happens when serving meets persecution? Well, the first thing that happens is **(1) (more) PERSECUTION**. It's in Acts 8:1, I promise. After the death of Stephen Luke then says, *"Now Saul was consenting to his death."* And look at the next sentence. *"At that time a great persecution arose against the church which was at Jerusalem; and they were all scattered throughout the regions of Judea and Samaria, except the Apostles.*

Go to verse three: *"As for Saul, he made havoc of the church, entering every house, and dragging off men and women, committing them to prison."*

Church, when you make up your mind to be a servant of the Lord, you can expect persecution on top of persecution. I mean, when you think it is over, don't think it's over for long because just as quickly as it stopped, it WILL start right back up again. And then – look at this – after you get more persecution, the second thing that happens when serving meets persecution is **(2) PANDEMONIUM**. Yeah, it gets crazy – when serving meets persecution. And it's in the text. It's in verse three and then it spreads from four – seven. It's in there. Verse three says, "As for Saul, he made havoc of the church, and dragging off men and women, committing them to prison." Church, can you not see the pandemonium that is going on in this verse? I mean, try to imagine your daddy being pulled off from the house by his feet. Imagine your momma being dragged off and thrown into prison. Imagine that. Imagine your sister, or your brother being dragged off. Can't you hear the cries? Can't you hear the screams? I can hear them. I can hear the hollering and the screams from loved ones. I can see the tears falling down the faces of children.

Somebody is trying to stop them; you know they are. It is pandemonium all over the city because the new force in town is fighting everyone who is on the Lord's side! It's pandemonium! It is a wild uproar going on. It is unrestrained disorder going on. And that is what pandemonium is. It is utter chaos. And pandemonium happens every time serving meets persecution because somebody is always fighting against the Lord and against the Lord's work!

But let me give this to you. Let me lay this in your lap this morning. I see at least two kinds of pandemonium in the text. I see a **PERFIDIOUS PANDEMONIUM**, and I see a **PROPHETIC PANDEMONIUM**. And I hope you see them, too. Check this out:

Perfidious means deliberately faithless; treacherous; deceitful. And that is exactly what Saul instituted. Luke says Saul *made* havoc. That is, Saul did not just persecute the church, but rather he intentionally began to destroy it.

The word used here is the same word that signifies the damage done by wild boars. This is utter demolition. This is destruction. This is devastation. You've got to see this.

Saul built and led a grass-roots effort. He went house-to-house. He didn't just arrest folks, but he dragged them out of their own houses, and I believe this led to **PERFIDIOUS PANDEMONIUM**. But check this out: whenever you find perfidious pandemonium, the Christian knows that on the other side of that is always **PROPHETIC PANDEMONIUM**. Where is it in the text? Well, it's implied because Luke says that because of this (because of the perfidious pandemonium) *"those who were scattered went everywhere preaching the Word"* (verse four). And it says (verse five) *"Then Philip went down to the city of Samaria and preached Christ to them."* And I know this ought to sound familiar to those of you who are reading along with me, because that is exactly what our Jesus said would happen – that is why it is prophetic. This is exactly what He said would happen at Acts 1:8. That is where Jesus said, "*But you shall receive power when the Holy Spirit has come upon you; and you shall be witnesses to Me in Jerusalem, and in all Judea, and in Samaria, and to the end of the earth!*"

And that Holy Ghost power showed up and He caused unclean spirits to cry with a loud voice, and they came out of many who were possessed! That Holy Ghost power showed up and He caused many who were paralyzed and many who were lame got up and were healed!

I can see the dismay in the crowd, but at least this time I know it was of the Lord! And since it was of the Lord — since it was a prophetic pandemonium, if I were there I would tell the crowd, "Be not dismayed, whatever betide – God will take care of you!

When serving meets persecution, **more persecution happens**, and **pandemonium happens (perfidious and prophetic)**, and then lastly, **(3) PLEASURE** happens.

That's why you don't have to worry about it, because at the end of the day, and it is found in the text – it's in verse eight – joy will come. And joy is pleasure. This is a holy pleasure, but it is pleasure.

This is what I am trying to tell you today: when serving meets persecution, holes are filled; wrongs are righted; crookedness is made straight; downs are turned upward; frowns are made into smiles; fists become lifted hands; tightness is loosened. In other words, there will be a gladness of heart whenever serving meets persecution!

Can't He put running in your feet? Can't He put a clapping in your hand? Can't He put a smile on your face? The Lord will give your joy! When serving meets persecution, He will give you joy! Greater is He that is within you, than he that is in the world! Jesus can, and He will, give you joy (when your serving is met with persecution)! Just don't give up! Don't give in! Don't throw in the towel.

I know you are tired. I know you have been crying. But you just have to remember that weeping may endure for a night, but joy – yes, it does – it comes in the morning! There will be some Sauls in your path. There will be some persecutors on your job. Persecutors are in your home. Persecutors are in your church. But just keep on serving!

I heard, a long time ago, somebody said, "I ain't gone let nobody turn me 'round!"

But I'm gonna keep on walking! I'm gonna keep on talking!

And that's because God deserves my service! God deserves all that I can do for Him! He has been SO good to me! So it doesn't matter how I am persecuted, I must always serve the Lord!

BIBLIOGRAPHY

BOOKS

Alexander, J.A. *The Acts of the Apostles*. Carlisle, Pennsylvania: The Banner of Truth Trust, 1875.

Allen, Kerry James. *Spurgeon's Quotes: The Definitive Collection*. The Woodland, Texas: Kress Biblical Resources, 2018.

Anyabwile, Thabiti M. *Finding Faithful Elders and Deacons*. Wheaton, Illinois: Crossway, 2012.

Barker, Kenneth, and John Kohlenberger III. *NIV Commentary: Volume 2: New Testament*. Grand Rapids, Michigan: Zondervan Publishing House, 1994.

Barnes, Frank, L. *The Office of Deacons*. Comp. *Church Membership Orientation for Baptist Churches*. Spokane: Pines Baptist Church, n.d.

Barnett, James Monroe. *The Diaconate: A Full and Equal Order: A Comprehensive and Critical Study of the Origin, Development, and Decline of the Diaconate in the Context*. Valley Forge, PA: Trinity Press International, 1983.

Bell, D.G., Ed. *The Newlight Baptist Journals of James Manning and James Innis.* Hantsport, NS: Lancelot Press, 1984.

Bercot, David W., Ed. *A Dictionary of Early Christian Beliefs.* Peabody, Mass: Hendrickson Pub., 1998.

Betteson, Henry, Ed. and trans. *The Early Christian Fathers.* London: Oxford, 1956.

Beverley, James and Barry M. Moody, Eds. *The Life and Journal of the Rev. Mr. Henry Alline.* Hantsport, NS: Lancelot Press, 1982.

Boice, James Montgomery. *Christ's Call to Discipleship.* Chicago: Moody Press, 1986.

Brackney, William H. *A Genetic History of Baptist Thought.* Macon, GA: Mercer University Press, 2004.

Brand, Chad Owen, and R. Stanton Norman. *Perspectives on Church Government: Five Views of Church Polity.* Nashville: Broadman and Holman, 2004.

Brown, J. Newton. *The Baptist Church Manual.* Philadelphia: American Baptist Publication Society, 1853.

Bruce, F.F. *The Acts of the Apostles: Greek Text with Introduction and Commentary.* 3rd ed. Grand Rapids: William B. Eerdmans Publishing Company, 1990.

Burroughs, P. E. *Honoring the Deaconship.* Nashville: Sunday School Board of the Southern Baptist Convention, 1929.

Conybeare, W.J. and Howson, J. S. *The Life and Epistles of St. Paul.* Grand Rapids, Michigan: William B. Eerdmans Pub. Co., 1855.

Cranfield, C. E. B. "Diakonia in the New Testament." Chapter in *Service in Christ: Essays Presented to Karl Barth on His 80th*

Birthday. Edited by James I. McCord and T. H. L. Parker. Grand Rapids: William B. Eerdmans Pub. Co., 1966.

Cuthbertson, Brian C., Ed. *The Journal of the Reverend John Payzant (1749-1834)*. Hantsport, NS: Lancelot Press, 1981.

Daniélou, Jean. *The Development of Christian Doctrine Before the Council of Nicea*. Trans. J.

Baker. London: Darton, Longman & Todd, 1964.

Dever, Mark. *Nine Marks of a Healthy Church*. expanded ed. Wheaton, IL: Crossway, 2004.

Dever, Mark, and Paul Alexander. *The Deliberate Church: Building Your Ministry on the Gospel*. Wheaton, IL: Crossway, 2005.

Deweese, Charles W. *The Emerging Role of Deacons*, 12–13. Nashville, Tennessee: Broadman Press, 1979.

Di Berardino, A., Ed. *Encyclopedia of the Early Church*. Cambridge: James Clarke, 1992.

Dobbins, Gaines S. *The Meaning of Ordination, Church Administration*, December 1960.

Dobbins, Gaines S. *Baptist Churches in Action: A Study of New Testament Principles and Modern Methods of Application*. Nashville: Sunday School Board, 1929.

Dresselhaus, Richard. *Deacon Ministry*. Springfield, Missouri: Gospel Publishing House, 1973.

Echlin, Edward. *The Deacon in the Church - Past and Future*. New York: Alba House, 1971.

Edgemon, Roy and Sneed, Barry, *Jesus by Heart: God Can Transform You to Be Like Jesus,* Nashville: LifeWay Press, 1999, 10.

Eims, Leroy. *Disciples in Action*. Wheaton, Illinois: Victor Books, 1981.

Engle, Paul E., and Steven B. Cowan, eds. *Who Runs the Church? 4 Views on Church Government*. Grand Rapids: Zondervan, 2004.

Ferguson, E., Ed. *Encyclopedia of Early Christianity*. NY: Garland, 1990.

Fickett, Harold L. Jr. *A Layman's Guide to Baptist Belief*. Michigan: Zondervan, 1965.

Fisher, Fred L., *Falling Walls: The Doctrine of Reconciliation*. Nashville: Convention, 1971, 62-63.

Fitzgerald, A. D., Ed. *Augustine Through the Ages: An Encyclopedia*. Grand Rapids, MI: Eerdmans, 1999.

Foshee, Howard B. *Now that You're a Deacon*. Nashville, Tennessee: Broadman, 1975.

Foshee, Howard B. *The Ministry of the Deacon*. Nashville: Convention, 1968, 35-36.

Foster, Richard J., *Celebration of Discipline: The Path to Spiritual Growth*. New York: Harper & Row, 1978,15.

Frank, Harry Thomas, editor. *Hammond's Atlas of the Bible Lands*. Wheaton, Illinois: Scripture Press Publications, 1977.

Freedman, David Noel. *The Anchor Bible Dictionary*. New York: Doubleday, 1992.

Frend, W.H.C. *The Early Church: From the Beginnings to 461*. London: SCM, 1992.

Gaebelein, Arno C. *The Acts of the Apostles*. Neptune, New Jersey: Loizeaux Brothers, 1912.

Gordon, Grant. *From Slavery to Freedom: The Life of David George, Pioneer Black Baptist Minister.* Hantsport, NS: Lancelot Press, 1992.

Greenleaf, Robert K., *Servant Leadership: A Journey into the Nature of Legitimate Power and Greatness.* New York: Paulist, 1977, 9-10.

Greenslade, S.L. Ed. *Early Latin Theology: The Library of Christian Classics, vol. 5.* Philadelphia: Westminster, 1956.

Gregory, L. A. *Baptist Convention of Ontario and Quebec Year Book, 1961-1962.* Toronto, ON: 1962.

Griffin-Allwood, Philip G. A., George A. Rawlyk and Jarold K. Zeman. *Baptists in Canada 1760-1990: A Bibliography of Selected Printed Resources in English.* Hantsport, NS: Lancelot Press, 1989.

Grillmeier, Aloys. *Christ in Christian Tradition.* Atlanta: John Knox, 1987.

Harnack, Adolf von. *History of Dogma.* NY: Dover: 1961.

Hartley, Bill. *When Deacons Deak. The Deacon*6, no. 3. April, May, June 1972, 24-25.

Heading, John. *Acts: A Study in New Testament Christianity.* Kansas City, Kansas: Walterick Publishers.

Henderson, J.T., *The Office of Deacon.* Knoxville: n.p., 1928.

Hiebert, D. Edmond. *Personalities Around Paul.* Chicago, Illinois: Moody Press, 1973.

Hirsch, Alan, *The Forgotten Ways: Reactivating the Missional Church.* Grand Rapids: Brazos Press, 2006.

Hiscox, Edward T. *The Hiscox Guide for Baptist Churches.* Valley Forge, PA: Judson Press, 1981.

Hobbs, H. H., *Ordination, Encyclopedia of Southern Baptists.* Nashville: Broadman, 1958, 2:1057.

Hobbs, James Rudolph. *The Pastor's Manual.* Nashville: Broadman Press, 1934.

Hopper, J. E. *Manual for Baptist Churches.* Saint John, 1894.

Howell, RBC. *The Deaconship: It's Nature, Qualifications, Relations & Duties.* Philadelphia: American Baptist Publication Society, 1846.

Ironside, H. A. *Lectures on the Book of Acts.* Neptune, New Jersey: Loizeaux Brothers, 1943.

Jenkens, Charles A. *Baptist Doctrines.* St. Louis: Chancy R. Barns, 1885.

Jensen, Irving L. *Acts: An Inductive Study.* Chicago, Illinois: Moody Press, 1968.

Johnson, Gordon G. *My Church: Manual of Baptist Faith and Action.* Evanston, Il: Harvest Publications, 1973.

Jones, R. Wayne. *The Dirty Feet People: Developing a Deacon Ministry that Will Grow Your Sunday School, Your Church, and Assimilate Those Whom You Have Reached.* Franklin, TN.: Growth Points Pub., 1993.

Jourard, Sidney M., *The Transparent Self.* New York: D. Van Nostrand, 1971.

Jurgens, William A., Ed. *Faith of the Early Fathers.* Collegeville, MN: Liturgical, 1970.

Kaiser, John Edmund, *Winning on Purpose: How to Organize Congregations to Succeed in Their Mission.* Nashville, TN: Abingdon, 2006.

Kelly, J.N.D. *Early Christian Doctrines.* San Francisco: Harper & Row, 1978.

Kelly, William. *An Exposition of the Acts of the Apostles.* Addison, Illinois: Bible Truth Publishers, 1890.

Kent, Homer A., Jr. *Jerusalem to Rome: Studies in the Book of Acts.* Grand Rapids: Baker Book House, 1974.

Larson, Bruce, *No Longer Strangers.* Waco: Word, 1971, 52.

Love, E. K. *History of the First African Baptist Church.* Savanah: Morning News Print, 1888.

MacArthur, John F. Jr. *The Gospel According to Jesus.* Grand Rapids: Zondervan Publishing House, 1988.

MacGregor, G. H. C. *Acts of the Apostles.* George Arthur Buttrick, ed. *The Interpreter's Bible.* Nashville: Abingdon Press, 1954.

Mainous, Charles E. *What on Earth is a Deacon?* Revised. Columbus, OH: Fundamental Baptist Publications, 1971, 1985.

Maring, Norman H. and. Hudson, Winthrop S. *A Baptist Manual of Polity and Practice: Revised Edition.* Valley Forge: The Judson Press, 1991.

Maston, T. B., *Why Live the Christian Life?* Nashville: Broadman, 1974, 138

Massey, Floyd, Jr. and McKinney, Samuel Berry. *Church Administration in the Black Perspective.* Valley Forge: Judson Press, 1976.

McBeth, H. Leon, *The Baptist Heritage: Four Centuries of Baptist Witness.* Nashville, TN: Broadman, 1987.

McCall, Duke K. Ed. *What is the Church?* Nashville: Broadman Press, 1958.

McGrath, Alister. *Evangelicalism and the Future of Christianity.* InterVarsity: Illinois, 1995.

McKeever, Joe. *Help! I'm a Deacon!* Cleveland, Tennessee: Parson's Porch & Company, 2015.

McKee, Elsie Anne. *John Calvin: On the Diaconate and Liturgical Almsgiving.* Geneva: Librairie Droz S.A., 1984.

McMickle, Marvin A. *Deacons in Today's Black Baptist Church.* Valley Forge, Pennsylvania: Judson, 2010.

McNeil, Jesse Jai. *Minister's Service Book for Pulpit and Parish.* Grand Rapids: William B. Eerdmans Publishing Company, 1961.

Monfalcone, Wesley R. *Counseling – Who Needs It?" The Deacon* 6, no. 3. April, May, June 1976: 12-14.

Morgan, G. Campbell. *The Acts of the Apostles.* Old Tappan, New Jersey: Fleming H. Revell Co., 1924.

Morris, Hollis R. *Concerning the Deacon for Whom God Is Looking.* Oklahoma City: Baptist General Convention, nd.

Morris, Leon. *Deacon.* Everett F. Harrison, ed. *Baker's Dictionary of Theology.* Grand Rapid: Baker Book House, 1970.

Nichols, Harold. *The Work of the Deacon and Deaconess.* Valley Forge, PA: Judson Press, 1984.

Naylor, Robert E. *The Baptist Deacon.* Nashville, Tennessee: Broadman Press, 1955.

Newton, Phil A. *Elders in Congregational Life: Rediscovering the Biblical Model for Church Leadership.* Grand Rapids: Kregel, 2005.

Nichols, Harold. *The Work of the Deacon & Deaconess: Second Revised Edition,* 1–2. Valley Forge, PA: Judson Press, 1984.

O'Donnell, J. D. *Handbook for Deacons.* Nashville, Tennessee: Randall House, 1973.

Olson, Jeannine E. *One Ministry, Many Roles: Deacons and Deaconesses through the Centuries.* Saint Louis: Concordia, 1992.

Pedersen, Herb. *A Deacon Ministry That Works.* Produced by Sampson Ministry Resources, 1989. Distributed by Church Growth Institute. Videocassette and Workbook.

Piper, John. *Biblical Eldership.* Minneapolis: Desiring God Ministries, 1999.

Plater, Ormonde. *Many Servants: An Introduction to Deacons.* Cowley Publications, Cambridge, Massachusetts, 2004.

Powell, Fred. *A Biblical Deacon Ministry for Your Church: Biblical Truth or Baptist Tradition.* Moore, OK.: Communicator Ministries, Inc., 1991.

Priestley, David T., Ed. *A Fragile Stability: Definition and Redefinition of Maritime Baptist Identity.* Hantsport, NS: Lancelot Press, 1994.

Rackham, R. B. *The Acts of the Apostles.* Grand Rapids, Michigan: Baker Book House, 1901.

Richards, Lawrence O. *A Theology of Christian Education.* Grand Rapids: Zondervan Publishers, 1975.

Robertson, A. T. *Epochs in the Life of Paul.* Grand Rapids, Michigan: Baker Book House, 1909.

Robinson, J. Armitage. "Deacon and Deaconess." *Encyclopaedia Biblica.* New York: Macmillan, 1914.

Roland, Dewitt, *Who's Boss in the Church."* Unpublished manuscript in possession of original writer.

Rowatt, Wade. *Discovering and Developing Your Counseling Skills. The Deacon* 6, no. 3 (April, May, June 1976): 9-11.

Ryrie, Charles D. *The Acts of the Apostles.* Chicago, Illinois: Moody Press, 1961.

Schweizer, Eduard. *Church Order in the New Testament*. London: SCM, 1961.

Scroggie, W. Graham. *The Acts of the Apostles*. Grand Rapids, Michigan: Zondervan Publishing House, n.d.

Sheffield, Robert. *The Ministry of Baptist Deacons*. Nashville: Convention Press, 1990.

Smith, J. Alfred. *Deacons Upholding the Pastor's Arms*. Elgin, Illinois: The Progressive Baptist Publishing House, n.d.

Smith, T. C. *Acts*. Clifton J Allen, ed. *The Broadman Bible Commentary*. Nashville: Broadman Press, 1970.

Stevenson, Ed. J. and Frend, W.H.C. *New Eusebius: Documents Illustrative of the History of the Church to AD 337*. London; SPCK, 1987.

Strauch, Alexander. *The New Testament Deacon: The Church's Minister of Mercy*. Littleton, Colorado: Lewis & Roth Pub., 1992.

Thomas, Donald F. *The Deacon in a Changing Church*. Valley Forge: Judson Press, 1969.

Thomas, W. H. Griffith. *Outline Studies in the Act of the Apostles*. Grand Rapids, Michigan: William B. Eerdmans Publishing Co., 1956.

Treadway, Charles F. *How to Start the Deacon Family Ministry Plan*. *The Deacon* 5, no. 3 (April, May, June 1975): 11-12.

Vander Lugt, Herbert. *Your Church in a Changing World*. Grand Rapids: Radio Bible Class, 1983.

Vaughn, Curtis. *Acts*. Grand Rapids, Michigan: Zondervan Publishing House, 1974.

Vos, Howard F. *Beginnings in Bible Archeology*. Chicago, Illinois: Moody Press, 1973.

Warren, Gordon C. *Basic Baptist Beliefs*. Canadian Baptist Federation.

Webb, Henry. *Deacons – Servant Models of the Church*. Nashville, Tennessee: Broadman and Holman, 2001.

Webb, Henry. *Deacons Ministering as Partners*. comp. *Equipping Deacons as Partners in Ministry*. Nashville: Convention Press, 1985.

Wilkes, C. Gene, *My Identity in Christ* (Nashville: LifeWay Press, 1999), 61-62.

Willson, James M. (2015). The Deacon. London, England: Dalton House.

Commentaries

Burroughs, P. E. *Honoring the Deaconship*. Nashville: Sunday School Board of the Southern Baptist Convention, 1929.

Barker, Kenneth L. & Kohlenberger, John, III. *NIV Bible Commentary Volume 1: Old Testament*, Zondervan Publishing House, Grand Rapids, Michigan 1994.

Barker, Kenneth L. & Kohlenberger, John, III. *NIV Bible Commentary Volume 2: New Testament*, Zondervan Publishing House, Grand Rapids, Michigan 1994.

Bock, Darrell L., *Acts: Baker Exegetical Commentary of the New Testament*, Baker Academic, 2009.

Fernando, Ajith, *The NIV Application Commentary: Acts*. Zondervan 1998.

Hughes, R. Kent. *Acts: The Church Afire*, Crossway Books, Wheaton, Illinois, 1996.

MacArthur, John. *The MacArthur Bible Commentary*, Thomas Nelson 2005.

Dictionaries

Baker, Warren, and Carperter, Eugene *The Complete Wordstudy Dictionary, Old Testament.* AMG Publishers 2003.

Butler, Trent C. *Holman Bible Dictionary* Holman Bible Publishers, 1991.

Renn, Stephen D. *Expository Dictionary of Bible Words* Hendrickson Publishers Marketing, LLC. 2005.

Youngblood, Ronald F. *Nelson's New Illustrated Bible Dictionary* Thomas Nelson Publishers, 1985.

Surveys

Deacon Survey – Various Congregations of First West Florida Baptist District Association. Given on November 14, 18, 26, and 29, 2018, at the Baptist Center.

Deacon Survey – Church Survey. Pre-Survey, October 2, 2018, Greater Little Rock Baptist Church; Post-Survey, December 2, 2018. Greater Little Rock Baptist Church.

Articles

Campbell, Steve. "Healthy Deacon-Pastor Relationships." *Deacon Magazine*, Lifeway.

Grant, George. "The High Call of Service." Ligonier Ministries, the teaching fellowship of R. C. Sproul.

Piper, John. "Rethinking the Governance Structure at Bethlehem Baptist Church; a Biblical Examination of Key Terms." *Desiring God.*

Newton, Phil. "When Deacons 'Deacon.'" *Founders Ministry*, April 26, 2018

WEBSITES

Biblehub, Strong's Exhaustive Concordance. Accessed April 11, 2019. http://biblehub.com/greek/4337.htm.

Founders Ministries When Deacons "Deacon." https://founders.org/2018/04/26/when-deacons-deacon. Accessed October 6, 2018.

Graham, Ron. Husband and Wife: Ephesians 5:22-33. 2001. Accessed April 22, 2019. http://www.simplybible.com/f74i-eph-husband-and-wife.htm.

Historical John the Baptist Church History. http://historicjohn-thebaptist.blogspot.com/p/church- history.html. Accessed October 1, 2018.

Mowczko, Marg. Paul's Main Point in Ephesians 5:22-33. April 30, 2012. Accessed April 22, 2019. http://margmowczko.com/pauls-main-point-in-eph-5_22-33/.

Oxford University Press. Household codes. Accessed April 22, 2019. http://www.oxfordbiblicalstudies.com/article/opr/t94/e912.

Terry Grove Baptist Church History. http://www.ter-rygrovechurch.org/church-history.html. Accessed October 1, 2018.

ONLINE JOURNALS

Bradshaw, Paul F. 1983. "Liturgical Presidency in the Early Church." *Grove Liturgical Study*, 36 Bramcote: Grove Books.

Cardwell, Albert L. "Listen, Deacon, Listen!" *The Deacon* 8, no. 2 (January, February, March 1978): 23. 9 Marks Journal, Deacons: May – June 2010

Jamie Dunlop, "Deacons: Shock Absorbers and Servants," March 31, 2010, accessed August 23, 2018

Benjamin Merkle, "The Biblical Qualifications and Responsibilities of Deacons," March 31, 2010, accessed August 22, 2018

Matt Schmucker, "The Committee-Free, Task-Specific Deacon," April 28, 2010, accessed August 22, 2018

Matt Schmucker, "How to Separate Deacon Work from Elder Work," April 28, 2010, accessed August 23, 2019

Printed in the USA
CPSIA information can be obtained
at www.ICGtesting.com
LVHW092111010624
781994LV00001B/111